Antony and Cleopatra

William Shakespeare

Published by

Hawk Press
4836/24, Ansari Road, Daryaganj
New Delhi - 110 002
Phones: +91-11-23278618, +91-11-43667199
E-mail: thehawkpress@gmail.com
www.thehawkpress.com

ISBN: 978-93-88318-10-5

The Tragedy of Antony and Cleopatra

The Actors Name

MARK ANTONY :	
OCTAVIUS CAESAR	} triumvirs
LEPIDUS	
SEXTUS POMPEIUS	
DOMITIUS ENOBARBUS	
VENTIDIUS	
EROS	
SCARUS	} friends to Antony
DERCETAS	
DEMETRIUS	
PHILO	
MAECENAS	
AGRIPPA	
DOLABELLA	
PROCULEIUS	} friends to Caesar
THIDIAS	
GALLUS	
MENAS	
MENECRATES	} friends to Sextus Pompeius
VARRIUS	

TAURUS: General To Caesar
CANIDIUS: General To Antony
SILIUS: An Officer In Ventidius's Army
An Ambassador From Antony To Caesar

Alexas MARDIAN: AN EUNUCH RANNIUS LUCILIUS SELEUCUS DIOMEDES	attendants on Cleopatra

LAMPRIUS: A Soothsayer
A CLOWN
CLEOPATRA: Queen Of Egypt
OCTAVIA: Sister To Caesar, And Wife To Antony
CHARMIAN
IRAS
Officers, Soldiers, Messengers, Attendants

I. 1

Enter Demetrius and Philo.

PHILO: Nay, but this dotage of our General's
O'erflows the measure: those his goodly eyes,
That o'er the files and musters of the war
Have glow'd like plated Mars, now bend, now turn,
The office and devotion of their view
Upon a tawny front: his Captain's heart,
Which in the scuffles of great fights hath burst
The buckles on his breast, reneges all temper,
And is become the bellows and the fan
To cool a gipsy's lust.

Flourish. Enter Antony, Cleopatra, her Ladies, the Train, with Eunuchs fanning her.

Look, where they come:
Take but good note, and you shall see in him.
The triple pillar of the world transform'd
Into a strumpet's fool: behold and see.

CLEOPATRA: If it be love indeed, tell me how much.

ANTONY: There's beggary in the love that can be reckon'd.

CLEOPATRA: I'll set a bourn how far to be belov'd.

ANTONY: Then must thou needs find out new heaven, new earth.

Enter an Attendant.

Attendant: News, my good Lord, from Rome.

ANTONY: Grates me: the sum.

CLEOPATRA: Nay, hear them, Antony:
Fulvia perchance is angry; or, who knows,
If the scarce-bearded Caesar have not sent
His powerful mandate to you, 'Do this, or this;

Take in that kingdom, and enfranchise that;
Perform 't, or else we damn thee.'
ANTONY: How, my love!
CLEOPATRA: Perchance! nay, and most like:
You must not stay here longer, your dismission
Is come from Caesar; therefore hear it, Antony.
Where's Fulvia's process? Caesar's I would say, both?
Call in the messengers. As I am Egypt's Queen,
Thou blushest, Antony; and that blood of thine
Is Caesar's homager: else so thy cheek pays shame
When shrill-tongued Fulvia scolds. The messengers!
ANTONY: Let Rome in Tiber melt, and the wide arch
Of the rang'd empire fall! Here is my space.
Kingdoms are clay: our dungy earth alike
Feeds beast as man: the nobleness of life
Is to do thus; when such a mutual pair
And such a twain can do't, in which I bind,
On pain of punishment, the world to weet
We stand up peerless.
CLEOPATRA: Excellent falsehood!
Why did he marry Fulvia, and not love her?
I'll seem the fool I am not; Antony
Will be himself.
ANTONY: But stirr'd by Cleopatra.
Now, for the love of Love and her soft hours,
Let's not confound the time with conference harsh:
There's not a minute of our lives should stretch
Without some pleasure now. What sport tonight?
CLEOPATRA: Hear the ambassadors.
ANTONY: Fie, wrangling Queen!
Whom every thing becomes, to chide, to laugh,
To weep; whose every passion fully strives
To make itself, in thee, fair and admired!
No messenger, but thine; and all alone

To-night we'll wander through the streets and note
The qualities of people. Come, my Queen;
Last night you did desire it: speak not to us.
Exeunt Antony and Cleopatra with their train.
DEMETRIUS: Is Caesar with Antonius priz'd so slight?
PHILO: Sir, sometimes, when he is not Antony,
He comes too short of that great property
Which still should go with Antony.
DEMETRIUS: I am full sorry
That he approves the common liar, who
Thus speaks of him at Rome: but I will hope
Of better deeds to-morrow. Rest you happy!
Exeunt.

I. 2

Enter Charmian, Iras, Alexas and a Soothsayer.

CHARMIAN: Lord Alexas, sweet Alexas, most any thing Alexas, almost most absolute Alexas, where's the soothsayer that you praised so to the Queen? O, that I knew this husband, which you say, must change his horns with garlands!

ALEXAS: Soothsayer!
Soothsayer: Your will?
CHARMIAN: Is this the man? Is't you, sir, that know things?
Soothsayer: In nature's infinite book of secrecy
A little I can read.
ALEXAS: Show him your hand.
Enter Domitius Enobarbus.
DOMITIUS: Bring in the banquet quickly; wine enough
Cleopatra's health to drink.
CHARMIAN: Good sir, give me good fortune.
Soothsayer: I make not, but foresee.
CHARMIAN: Pray, then, foresee me one.

Soothsayer: You shall be yet far fairer than you are.

CHARMIAN: He means in flesh.

IRAS: No, you shall paint when you are old.

CHARMIAN: Wrinkles forbid!

ALEXAS: Vex not his prescience; be attentive.

CHARMIAN: Hush!

Soothsayer: You shall be more beloving than beloved.

CHARMIAN: I had rather heat my liver with drinking.

ALEXAS: Nay, hear him.

CHARMIAN: Good now, some excellent fortune! Let me be married to three kings in a forenoon, and widow them all: let me have a child at fifty, to whom Herod of Jewry may do homage: find me to marry me with Octavius Caesar, and companion me with my mistress.

Soothsayer: You shall outlive the Lady whom you serve.

CHARMIAN: O excellent! I love long life better than figs.

Soothsayer: You have seen and proved a fairer former fortune Than that which is to approach.

CHARMIAN: Then belike my children shall have no names: prithee, how many boys and wenches must I have?

Soothsayer: If every of your wishes had a womb.
And fertile every wish, a million.

CHARMIAN: Out, fool! I forgive thee for a witch.

ALEXAS: You think none but your sheets are privy to your wishes.

CHARMIAN: Nay, come, tell Iras hers.

ALEXAS: We'll know all our fortunes.

DOMITIUS: Mine, and most of our fortunes, to-night, shall be drunk to bed.

IRAS: There's a palm presages chastity, if nothing else.

CHARMIAN: E'en as the o'erflowing Nilus presageth

famine.

IRAS: Go, you wild bedfellow, you cannot soothsay.

CHARMIAN: Nay, if an oily palm be not a fruitful prognostication, I cannot scratch mine ear. Prithee, tell her but a worky-day fortune.

Soothsayer: Your fortunes are alike.

IRAS: But how, but how? Give me particulars.

Soothsayer: I have said.

IRAS: Am I not an inch of fortune better than she?

CHARMIAN: Well, if you were but an inch of fortune better than I, where would you choose it?

IRAS: Not in my husband's nose.

CHARMIAN: Our worser thoughts heavens mend!

Alexas: Come, his fortune, his fortune! O, let him marry a woman that cannot go, sweet Isis, I beseech thee! and let her die too, and give him a worse! and let worst follow worse, till the worst of all follow him laughing to his grave, fifty-fold a cuckold! Good Isis, hear me this prayer, though thou deny me a matter of more weight; good Isis, I beseech thee!

IRAS: Amen. Dear Goddess, hear that prayer of the people! for, as it is a heartbreaking to see a handsome man loose-wiv'd, so it is a deadly sorrow to behold a foul knave uncuckolded: therefore, dear Isis, keep decorum, and fortune him accordingly!

CHARMIAN: Amen.

ALEXAS: Lo, now, if it lay in their hands to make me a cuckold, they would make themselves whores, but they'ld do't!

DOMITIUS: Hush! here comes Antony.

CHARMIAN: Not he; the Queen.

Enter Cleopatra.

CLEOPATRA: Saw you, my Lord?

DOMITIUS: No, Lady.

CLEOPATRA: Was he not here?

CHARMIAN: No, Madam.

CLEOPATRA: He was disposed to mirth; but on the sudden A Roman thought hath struck him. Domitius!

DOMITIUS: Madam?

CLEOPATRA: Seek him, and bring him hither.
Where's Alexas?

ALEXAS: Here, at your service. My Lord approaches.

CLEOPATRA: We will not look upon him: go with us.

Exeunt.

Enter Antony with a Messenger and Attendants.

Messenger: Fulvia thy wife first came into the field.

ANTONY: Against my brother Lucius?

Messenger: Ay: but soon that war had end,
And the time's state
Made friends of them, joining their force 'gainst Caesar;
Whose better issue in the war, from Italy,
Upon the first encounter, drave them.

ANTONY: Well, what worst?

Messenger: The nature of bad news infects the teller.

ANTONY: When it concerns the fool or coward. On:
Things that are past are done with me. 'Tis thus:
Who tells me true, though in his tale lie death,
I hear him as he flatter'd.

Messenger: Labienus—
This is stiff news—hath, with his Parthian force,
Extended Asia from Euphrates;
His conquering banner shook from Syria
To Lydia and to Ionia; whilst—

ANTONY: Antony, thou wouldst say—

Messenger: O, my Lord!

ANTONY: Speak to me home, mince not the general tongue:
Name Cleopatra as she is call'd in Rome;

Rail thou in Fulvia's phrase; and taunt my faults
With such full licence as both truth and malice
Have power to utter. O, then we bring forth weeds,
When our quick minds lie still; and our ills told us
Is as our earing. Fare thee well awhile.

Messenger: At your noble pleasure.

Exit.

ANTONY: From Sicyon, how the news! Speak there!

First Attendant: The man from Sicyon—is there such an one?

Second Attendant: He stays upon your will.

ANTONY: Let him appear.
These strong Egyptian fetters I must break,
Or lose myself in dotage.
Enter another Messenger.
What are you?

Second Messenger: Fulvia, thy wife is dead.

ANTONY: Where died she?

Second Messenger: In Sicyon:
Her length of sickness, with what else more serious
Importeth thee to know, this bears.

ANTONY: Forbear me.
Exeunt Messenger.
There's a great spirit gone! Thus did I desire it:
What our contempt doth often hurl from us,
We wish it ours again; the present pleasure,
By revolution low'ring, does become
The opposite of itself: she's good, being gone;
The hand could pluck her back that shov'd her on.
I must from this enchanting Queen break off:
Ten thousand harms, more than the ills I know,
My idleness doth hatch. How now! Enobarbus!
Enter Domitius Enobarbus.

DOMITIUS: What's your pleasure, sir?

ANTONY: I must with haste from hence.

DOMITIUS: Why, then, we kill all our women: we see how mortal an unkindness is to them; if they suffer our departure, death's the word.

ANTONY: I must be gone.

DOMITIUS: Under a compelling occasion, let women die; it were pity to cast them away for nothing; though, between them and a great cause, they should be esteemed nothing. Cleopatra, catching but the least noise of this, dies instantly; I have seen her die twenty times upon far poorer moment: I do think there is mettle in death, which commits some loving act upon her, she hath such a celerity in dying.

ANTONY: She is cunning past man's thought.

Exit Alexas.

DOMITIUS: Alack, sir, no; her passions are made of nothing but the finest part of pure love: we cannot call her winds and waters, sighs and tears; they are greater storms and tempests than almanacs can report: this cannot be cunning in her; if it be, she makes a shower of rain as well as Jove.

ANTONY: Would I had never seen her.

DOMITIUS: O, sir, you had then left unseen a wonderful piece of work; which not to have been blest withal would have discredited your travel.

ANTONY: Fulvia is dead.

DOMITIUS: Sir?

ANTONY: Fulvia is dead.

DOMITIUS: Fulvia!

ANTONY: Dead.

DOMITIUS: Why, sir, give the gods a thankful sacrifice. When it pleaseth their deities to take the wife of a man from him, it shows to man the tailors of the earth; comforting therein, that when old robes are worn out, there are members to make new. If there were no more women but Fulvia, then had you indeed a cut, and the case to be lamented: this grief is crown'd with consolation; your old smock brings forth a new petticoat: and indeed the tears live in an onion that should water this sorrow.

ANTONY: The business she hath broached in the State
Cannot endure my absence.

DOMITIUS: And the business you have broached here cannot be without you; especially that of Cleopatra's, which wholly depends on your abode.

ANTONY: No more light answers. Let our officers
Have notice what we purpose. I shall break
The cause of our expedience to the Queen,
And get her leave to part. For not alone
The death of Fulvia, with more urgent touches,
Do strongly speak to us; but the letters too
Of many our contriving friends in Rome
Petition us at home: Sextus Pompeius
Hath given the dare to Caesar, and commands
The empire of the sea: our slippery people,
Whose love is never link'd to the deserver
Till his deserts are past, begin to throw
Pompey the Great and all his dignities
Upon his son; who, high in name and power,
Higher than both in blood and life, stands up
For the main soldier: whose quality, going on,
The sides o' th' world may danger: much is breeding,
Which, like the courser's hair, hath yet but life,
And not a serpent's poison. Say, our pleasure,
To such whose place is under us, requires
Our quick remove from hence.

DOMITIUS: I shall do't.

Exeunt.

I. 3

Enter Cleopatra, Charmian, Iras and Alexas.

CLEOPATRA: Where is he?

CHARMIAN: I did not see him since.

CLEOPATRA: See where he is, who's with him, what he does:
I did not send you: if you find him sad,
Say I am dancing; if in mirth, report
That I am sudden sick: quick, and return.
Exit Alexas.

CHARMIAN: Madam, methinks, if you did love him dearly, You do not hold the method to enforce The like from him.

CLEOPATRA: What should I do, I do not?

CHARMIAN: In each thing give him way, cross him in nothing.

CLEOPATRA: Thou teachest like a fool; the way to lose him.

CHARMIAN: Tempt him not so too far; I wish, forbear:
In time we hate that which we often fear.
But here comes Antony.
Enter Antony.

CLEOPATRA: I am sick and sullen.

ANTONY: I am sorry to give breathing to my purpose.

CLEOPATRA: Help me away, dear Charmian; I shall fall:
It cannot be thus long, the sides of Nature
Will not sustain it.

ANTONY: Now, my dearest Queen,—

CLEOPATRA: Pray you, stand father from me.

ANTONY: What's the matter?

CLEOPATRA: I know, by that same eye, there's some good news.
What says the married woman? You may go:

Would she had never given you leave to come!
Let her not say 'tis I that keep you here:
I have no power upon you; hers you are.
ANTONY: The gods best know, –
CLEOPATRA: O, never was there Queen
So mightily betray'd! yet at the first
I saw the treasons planted.
ANTONY: Cleopatra, –
CLEOPATRA: Why should I think you can be mine and true,
Though you in swearing shake the throned gods,
Who have been false to Fulvia? Riotous madness,
To be entangled with those mouth-made vows,
Which break themselves in swearing!
ANTONY: Most sweet Queen, –
CLEOPATRA: Nay, pray you, seek no colour for your going,
But bid farewell, and go: when you sued staying,
Then was the time for words: no going then;
Eternity was in our lips and eyes,
Bliss in our brows' bent; none our parts so poor,
But was a race of heaven: they are so still,
Or thou, the greatest soldier of the world,
Art turn'd the greatest liar.
ANTONY: How now, Lady!
CLEOPATRA: I would I had thy inches; thou shouldst know There were a heart in Egypt.
ANTONY: Hear me, Queen:
The strong necessity of time commands
Our services awhile; but my full heart
Remains in use with you. Our Italy
Shines o'er with civil swords: Sextus Pompeius
Makes his approaches to the port of Rome:
Equality of two domestic powers
Breed scrupulous faction: the hated, grown to

strength,
Are newly grown to love: the condemn'd Pompey,
Rich in his father's honour, creeps apace,
Into the hearts of such, as have not thrived
Upon the present state, whose numbers threaten;
And quietness, grown sick of rest, would purge
By any desperate change: my more particular,
And that which most with you should safe my going,
Is Fulvia's death.

CLEOPATRA: Though age from folly could not give me freedom,
It does from childishness: can Fulvia die?

ANTONY: She's dead, my Queen:
Look here, and at thy sovereign leisure read
The garboils she awak'd; at the last, best:
See when and where she died.

CLEOPATRA: O most false love!
Where be the sacred vials thou shouldst fill
With sorrowful water? Now I see, I see,
In Fulvia's death, how mine receiv'd shall be.

ANTONY: Quarrel no more, but be prepar'd to know
The purposes I bear; which are, or cease,
As you shall give the advice. By the fire
That quickens Nilus' slime, I go from hence
Thy soldier, servant; making peace or war
As thou affect'st.

CLEOPATRA: Cut my lace, Charmian, come;
But let it be: I am quickly ill, and well,
So Antony loves.

ANTONY: My precious Queen, forbear;
And give true evidence to his love, which stands
An honourable trial.
CLEOPATRA: So Fulvia told me.
I prithee, turn aside and weep for her,
Then bid adieu to me, and say the tears
Belong to Egypt: good now, play one scene
Of excellent dissembling; and let it look
Life perfect honour.
ANTONY: You'll heat my blood: no more.
CLEOPATRA: You can do better yet; but this is meetly.
ANTONY: Now, by my sword –
CLEOPATRA: And target. Still he mends;
But this is not the best. Look, prithee, Charmian,
How this Herculean Roman does become
The carriage of his chafe.
ANTONY: I'll leave you, Lady.
CLEOPATRA: Courteous Lord, one word.
Sir, you and I must part, but that's not it:
Sir, you and I have lov'd, but there's not it;
That you know well: something it is I would,
O, my oblivion is a very Antony,
And I am all forgotten.
ANTONY: But that your royalty
Holds idleness your subject, I should take you
For idleness itself.
CLEOPATRA: 'Tis sweating labour,
To bear such idleness so near the heart
As Cleopatra this. But, sir, forgive me;
Since my becomings kill me, when they do not
Eye well to you: your honour calls you hence;
Therefore be deaf to my unpitied folly.
And all the gods go with you! upon your sword
Sit laurel victory! and smooth success
Be strew'd before your feet!

ANTONY: Let us go. Come;
Our separation so abides, and flies,
That thou, residing here, go'st yet with me,
And I, hence fleeting, here remain with thee. Away!
Exeunt.

I. 4

Enter Caesar, reading a letter, Lepidus and their train.

CAESAR: You may see, Lepidus, and henceforth know,
It is not Caesar's natural vice to hate
Our great competitor: from Alexandria
This is the news: he fishes, drinks, and wastes
The lamps of night in revel; is not more man-like
Than Cleopatra; nor the queen of Ptolemy
More womanly than he; hardly gave audience, or
Vouchsaf'd to think he had partners: you shall find there
A man who is the abstract of all faults
That all men follow.

LEPIDUS: I must not think there are
Evils enow to darken all his goodness:
His faults in him seem as the spots of heaven,
More fiery by night's blackness; hereditary,
Rather than purchased; what he cannot change,
Than what he chooses.

CAESAR: You are too indulgent. Let us grant, it is not
Amiss to tumble on the bed of Ptolemy;
To give a kingdom for a mirth; to sit
And keep the turn of tippling with a slave;
To reel the streets at noon, and stand the buffet
With knaves that smell of sweat: say this becomes him–
As his composure must be rare indeed
Whom these things cannot blemish–yet must Antony

No way excuse his soils, when we do bear
So great weight in his lightness. If he fill'd
His vacancy with his voluptuousness,
Full surfeits, and the dryness of his bones,
Call on him for't: but to confound such time,
That drums him from his sport, and speaks as loud
As his own state and ours—'tis to be chid
As we rate boys, who, being mature in knowledge,
Pawn their experience to their present pleasure,
And so rebel to judgment.
Enter a Messenger.
LEPIDUS: Here's more news.
Messenger: Thy biddings have been done; and every hour,
Most noble Caesar, shalt thou have report
How 'tis abroad. Pompey is strong at sea;
And it appears he is belov'd of those
That only have fear'd Caesar: to the ports
The discontents repair, and men's reports
Give him much wrong'd.
CAESAR: I should have known no less.
It hath been taught us from the primal state,
That he which is, was wish'd until he were;
And the ebb'd man, ne'er loved till ne'er worth love,
Comes fear'd by being lack'd. This common body,
Like to a vagabond flag upon the stream,
Goes to and back, lackeying the varying tide,
To rot itself with motion.
Messenger: Caesar, I bring thee word,
Menecrates and Menas, famous pirates,
Make the sea serve them, which they ear and wound
With keels of every kind: many hot inroads
They make in Italy; the borders maritime
Lack blood to think on't, and flush youth revolt:
No vessel can peep forth, but 'tis as soon

Taken as seen; for Pompey's name strikes more
Than could his war resisted.
CAESAR: Antony,
Leave thy lascivious wassails. When thou once
Wast beaten from Modena, where thou slew'st
Hirtius and Pansa, Consuls, at thy heel
Did famine follow; whom thou fought'st against,
Though daintily brought up, with patience more
Than savages could suffer: thou didst drink
The stale of horses, and the gilded puddle
Which beasts would cough at: thy palate then did deign
The roughest berry on the rudest hedge;
Yea, like the stag, when snow the pasture sheets,
The barks of trees thou browsed'st; on the Alps
It is reported thou didst eat strange flesh,
Which some did die to look on: and all this—
It wounds thine honour that I speak it now—
Was borne so like a soldier, that thy cheek
So much as lank'd not.
LEPIDUS: 'Tis pity of him.
CAESAR: Let his shames quickly
Drive him to Rome: 'tis time we twain
Did show ourselves i' th' field; and to that end
Assemble we immediate council: Pompey
Thrives in our idleness.
LEPIDUS: To-morrow, Caesar,
I shall be furnish'd to inform you rightly
Both what by sea and land I can be able
To front this present time.
CAESAR: Till which encounter,
It is my business too. Farewell.
LEPIDUS: Farewell, my lord: what you shall know meantime
Of stirs abroad, I shall beseech you, sir,

To let me be partaker.
CAESAR: Doubt not, sir;
I knew it for my bond.
Exeunt.

I. 5

Enter Cleopatra, Charmian, Iras and Mardian.

CLEOPATRA: Charmian!
CHARMIAN: Madam?
CLEOPATRA: Ha, ha!
Give me to drink mandragora.
CHARMIAN: Why, Madam?
CLEOPATRA: That I might sleep out this great gap of time
My Antony is away.
CHARMIAN: You think of him too much.
CLEOPATRA: O, 'tis treason!
CHARMIAN: Madam, I trust, not so.
CLEOPATRA: Thou, eunuch Mardian!
MARDIAN: What's your Highness' pleasure?
CLEOPATRA: Not now to hear thee sing; I take no pleasure
In aught an eunuch has: 'tis well for thee,
That, being unseminar'd, thy freer thoughts
May not fly forth of Egypt. Hast thou affections?
MARDIAN: Yes, gracious Madam.
CLEOPATRA: Indeed!
MARDIAN: Not in deed, Madam; for I can do nothing
But what indeed is honest to be done:
Yet have I fierce affections, and think
What Venus did with Mars.
CLEOPATRA: O Charmian,
Where think'st thou he is now? Stands he, or sits he?
Or does he walk? or is he on his horse?
O happy horse, to bear the weight of Antony!

Do bravely, horse! for wot'st thou whom thou mov'st?
The demi-Atlas of this earth, the arm
And burgonet of men. He's speaking now,
Or murmuring 'Where's my serpent of old Nile?'
For so he calls me: now I feed myself
With most delicious poison. Think on me,
That am with Phoebus' amorous pinches black,
And wrinkled deep in time? Broad-fronted Caesar,
When thou wast here above the ground, I was
A morsel for a monarch: and great Pompey
Would stand and make his eyes grow in my brow;
There would he anchor his aspect and die
With looking on his life.

Enter Alexas.

ALEXAS: Sovereign of Egypt, hail!

CLEOPATRA: How much unlike art thou Mark Antony!
Yet, coming from him, that great medicine hath
With his tinct gilded thee.
How goes it with my brave Mark Antony?

ALEXAS: Last thing he did, dear Queen,
He kiss'd—the last of many doubled kisses—
This orient pearl. His speech sticks in my heart.

CLEOPATRA: Mine ear must pluck it thence.

ALEXAS: 'Good friend,' quoth he,
'Say, the firm Roman to great Egypt sends
This treasure of an oyster; at whose foot,
To mend the petty present, I will piece
Her opulent Throne with Kingdoms; all the east,
Say thou, shall call her mistress.' So he nodded,
And soberly did mount an arm-gaunt steed,
Who neigh'd so high, that what I would have spoke
Was beastly dumb'd by him.

CLEOPATRA: What, was he sad or merry?

ALEXAS: Like to the time o' th' year between the extremes
Of hot and cold, he was nor sad nor merry.
CLEOPATRA: O well-divided disposition! Note him,
Note him good Charmian, 'tis the man; but note him:
He was not sad, for he would shine on those
That make their looks by his; he was not merry,
Which seem'd to tell them his remembrance lay
In Egypt with his joy; but between both:
O heavenly mingle! Be'st thou sad or merry,
The violence of either thee becomes,
So does it no man else. Met'st thou my posts?
ALEXAS: Ay, Madam, twenty several messengers:
Why do you send so thick?
CLEOPATRA: Who's born that day
When I forget to send to Antony,
Shall die a beggar. Ink and paper, Charmian.
Welcome, my good Alexas. Did I, Charmian,
Ever love Caesar so?
CHARMIAN: O that brave Caesar!
CLEOPATRA: Be chok'd with such another emphasis!
Say, the brave Antony.
CHARMIAN: The valiant Caesar!
CLEOPATRA: By Isis, I will give thee bloody teeth,
If thou with Caesar paragon again
My man of men.
CHARMIAN: By your most gracious pardon,
I sing but after you.
CLEOPATRA: My salad days,
When I was green in judgment: cold in blood,
To say as I said then! But, come, away;
Get me ink and paper:
He shall have every day a several greeting,
Or I'll unpeople Egypt.

Exeunt.

II. 1

Enter Pompey, Menecrates and Menas, in warlike manner.

POMPEY: If the great gods be just, they shall assist
The deeds of justest men.
MENECRATES: Know, worthy Pompey,
That what they do delay, they not deny.
POMPEY: Whiles we are suitors to their throne, decays
The thing we sue for.
MENECRATES: We, ignorant of ourselves,
Beg often our own harms, which the wise powers
Deny us for our good; so find we profit
By losing of our prayers.
POMPEY: I shall do well:
The people love me, and the sea is mine;
My powers are crescent, and my auguring hope
Says it will come to the full. Mark Antony
In Egypt sits at dinner, and will make
No wars without doors: Caesar gets money where
He loses hearts: Lepidus flatters both,
Of both is flatter'd; but he neither loves,
Nor either cares for him.
MENAS: Caesar and Lepidus
Are in the field: a mighty strength they carry.
POMPEY: Where have you this? 'tis false.
MENAS: From Silvius, sir.
POMPEY: He dreams: I know they are in Rome together,
Looking for Antony. But all the charms of love,
Salt Cleopatra, soften thy wan'd lip!
Let witchcraft join with beauty, lust with both!
Tie up the libertine in a field of feasts,
Keep his brain fuming; Epicurean cooks
Sharpen with cloyless sauce his appetite;
That sleep and feeding may prorogue his honour

Even till a Lethe'd dullness!
How now, Varrius!

Enter Varrius.

VARRIUS: This is most certain that I shall deliver:
Mark Antony is every hour in Rome
Expected: since he went from Egypt, 'tis
A space for further travel.

POMPEY: I could have given less matter
A better ear. Menas, I did not think
This amorous surfeiter would have donn'd his helm
For such a petty war: his soldiership
Is twice the other twain: but let us rear
The higher our opinion, that our stirring
Can from the lap of Egypt's widow, pluck
The ne'er-lust-wearied Antony.

MENAS: I cannot hope
Caesar and Antony shall well greet together:
His wife that's dead did trespasses to Caesar;
His brother warr'd upon him; although, I think,
Not mov'd by Antony.

POMPEY: I know not, Menas,
How lesser enmities may give way to greater.
Were't not that we stand up against them all,
'Twere pregnant they should square between themselves;
For they have entertained cause enough
To draw their swords: but how the fear of us
May cement their divisions and bind up
The petty difference, we yet not know.
Be't as our gods will have't! It only stands
Our lives upon, to use our strongest hands.
Come, Menas.

Exeunt.

II. 2

Enter Domitius Enobarbus and Lepidus.

LEPIDUS: Good Enobarbus, 'tis a worthy deed,
And shall become you well, to entreat your captain
To soft and gentle speech.
DOMITIUS: I shall entreat him
To answer like himself: if Caesar move him,
Let Antony look over Caesar's head
And speak as loud as Mars. By Jupiter,
Were I the wearer of Antonius' beard,
I would not shave't to-day.
LEPIDUS: 'Tis not a time
For private stomaching.
DOMITIUS: Every time
Serves for the matter that is then born in't.
LEPIDUS: But small to greater matters must give way.
DOMITIUS: Not if the small come first.
LEPIDUS: Your speech is passion:
But, pray you, stir no embers up. Here comes
The noble Antony.
Enter Antony and Ventidius.
DOMITIUS: And yonder, Caesar.
Enter Caesar, Maecenas and Agrippa.
ANTONY: If we compose well here, to Parthia:
Hark, Ventidius.
CAESAR: I do not know, Maecenas; ask Agrippa.
LEPIDUS: Noble friends,
That which combined us was most great, and let not
A leaner action rend us. What's amiss,
May it be gently heard: when we debate
Our trivial difference loud, we do commit
Murder in healing wounds: then, noble partners,
The rather, for I earnestly beseech,
Touch you the sourest points with sweetest terms,
Nor curstness grow to the matter.

ANTONY: 'Tis spoken well.
Were we before our armies, and to fight.
I should do thus.
Flourish.
CAESAR: Welcome to Rome.
ANTONY: Thank you.
CAESAR: Sit.
ANTONY: Sit, sir.
CAESAR: Nay, then.
ANTONY: I learn, you take things ill which are not so,
Or being, concern you not.
CAESAR: I must be laugh'd at,
If, or for nothing or a little, I
Should say myself offended, and with you
Chiefly i' th' world; more laugh'd at, that I should
Once name you derogately, when to sound your name
It not concern'd me.
ANTONY: My being in Egypt, Caesar,
What was't to you?
CAESAR: No more than my residing here at Rome
Might be to you in Egypt: yet, if you there
Did practise on my State, your being in Egypt
Might be my question.
ANTONY: How intend you, practised?
CAESAR: You may be pleas'd to catch at mine intent
By what did here befal me. Your wife and brother
Made wars upon me; and their contestation
Was theme for you, you were the word of war.
ANTONY: You do mistake your business; my brother never
Did urge me in his act: I did inquire it;
And have my learning from some true reports,
That drew their swords with you. Did he not rather
Discredit my authority with yours;

And make the wars alike against my stomach,
Having alike your cause? Of this my letters
Before did satisfy you. If you'll patch a quarrel,
As matter whole you have not to make it with,
It must not be with this.
CAESAR: You praise yourself
By laying defects of judgment to me; but
You patch'd up your excuses.
ANTONY: Not so, not so;
I know you could not lack, I am certain on't,
Very necessity of this thought, that I,
Your partner in the cause 'gainst which he fought,
Could not with graceful eyes attend those wars
Which fronted mine own peace. As for my wife,
I would you had her spirit in such another:
The third o' th' world is yours; which with a snaffle
You may pace easy, but not such a wife.
DOMITIUS: Would we had all such wives, that the men might go to wars with the women!
ANTONY: So much uncurbable, her garboils, Caesar
Made out of her impatience, which not wanted
Shrewdness of policy too, I grieving grant,
Did you too much disquiet: for that you must
But say, I could not help it.
CAESAR: I wrote to you
When rioting in Alexandria; you
Did pocket up my letters, and with taunts
Did gibe my missive out of audience.
ANTONY: Sir,
He fell upon me ere admitted: then
Three kings I had newly feasted, and did want
Of what I was i' th' morning: but next day
I told him of myself; which was as much
As to have ask'd him pardon. Let this fellow
Be nothing of our strife; if we contend,

Out of our question wipe him.
CAESAR: You have broken
The article of your oath; which you shall never
Have tongue to charge me with.
LEPIDUS: Soft, Caesar!
ANTONY: No,
Lepidus, let him speak:
The honour is sacred which he talks on now,
Supposing that I lack'd it. But, on, Caesar;
The article of my oath.
CAESAR: To lend me arms and aid when I requir'd them;
The which you both denied.
ANTONY: Neglected, rather;
And then when poison'd hours had bound me up
From mine own knowledge. As nearly as I may,
I'll play the penitent to you: but mine honesty
Shall not make poor my greatness, nor my power
Work without it. Truth is, that Fulvia,
To have me out of Egypt, made wars here;
For which myself, the ignorant motive, do
So far ask pardon as befits mine honour
To stoop in such a case.
LEPIDUS: 'Tis noble spoken.
MAECENAS: If it might please you, to enforce no further
The griefs between ye: to forget them quite
Were to remember that the present need,
Speaks to atone you.
LEPIDUS: Worthily spoken, Maecenas.
DOMITIUS: Or, if you borrow one another's love for the instant, you may, when you hear no more words of Pompey, return it again: you shall have time to wrangle in when you have nothing else to do.
ANTONY: Thou art a soldier only: speak no more.

DOMITIUS: That truth should be silent I had almost forgot.
ANTONY: You wrong this presence; therefore speak no more.
DOMITIUS: Go to, then; your considerate stone.
CAESAR: I do not much dislike the matter, but
The manner of his speech; for't cannot be
We shall remain in friendship, our conditions
So differing in their acts. Yet if I knew
What hoop should hold us stanch, from edge to edge
O' the world, I would pursue it.
AGRIPPA: Give me leave, Caesar –
CAESAR: Speak, Agrippa.
AGRIPPA: Thou hast a sister by the mother's side,
Admired Octavia: great Mark Antony
Is now a widower.
CAESAR: Say not so, Agrippa:
If Cleopatra heard you, your reproof
Were well deserved of rashness.
ANTONY: I am not married, Caesar: let me hear
Agrippa further speak.
AGRIPPA: To hold you in perpetual amity,
To make you brothers, and to knit your hearts
With an unslipping knot, take Antony
Octavia to his wife; whose beauty claims
No worse a husband than the best of men;
Whose virtue and whose general graces, speak
That which none else can utter. By this marriage,
All little jealousies, which now seem great,
And all great fears, which now import their dangers,
Would then be nothing: truths would be tales,
Where now half tales be truths: her love to both,
Would, each to other and all loves to both,
Draw after her. Pardon what I have spoke;
For 'tis a studied, not a present thought,

By duty ruminated.
ANTONY: Will Caesar speak?
CAESAR: Not till he hears how Antony is touch'd
With what is spoke already.
ANTONY: What power is in Agrippa,
If I would say, 'Agrippa, be it so,'
To make this good?
CAESAR: The power of Caesar, and
His power unto Octavia.
ANTONY: May I never
To this good purpose, that so fairly shows,
Dream of impediment! Let me have thy hand:
Further this act of grace: and from this hour,
The heart of brothers govern in our loves,
And sway our great designs!
CAESAR: There is my hand.
A sister I bequeath you, whom no brother
Did ever love so dearly: let her live
To join our kingdoms and our hearts; and never
Fly off our loves again!
LEPIDUS: Happily, Amen!
ANTONY: I did not think to draw my sword 'gainst
Pompey;
For he hath laid strange courtesies and great
Of late upon me: I must thank him only,
Lest my remembrance suffer ill report;
At heel of that, defy him.
LEPIDUS: Time calls upon's:
Of us must Pompey presently be sought,
Or else he seeks out us.
ANTONY: Where lies he?
CAESAR: About the mount Misenum.
ANTONY: What is his strength by land?
CAESAR: Great and increasing: but by sea
He is an absolute master.

ANTONY: So is the fame.
Would we had spoke together! Haste we for it:
Yet, ere we put ourselves in arms, dispatch we
The business we have talk'd of.
CAESAR: With most gladness:
And do invite you to my sister's view,
Whither straight I'll lead you.
ANTONY: Let us, Lepidus,
Not lack your company.
LEPIDUS: Noble Antony,
Not sickness should detain me.
Flourish. Exeunt Caesar, Antony and Lepidus.
MAECENAS: Welcome from Egypt, sir.
DOMITIUS: Half the heart of Caesar, worthy Maecenas!
My honourable friend, Agrippa!
AGRIPPA: Good Enobarbus!
MAECENAS: We have cause to be glad that matters are so well digested. You stayed well by 't in Egypt.
DOMITIUS: Ay, sir; we did sleep day out of countenance, and made the night light with drinking.
MAECENAS: Eight wild-boars roasted whole at a breakfast, and but twelve persons there; is this true?
DOMITIUS: This was but as a fly by an eagle: we had much more monstrous matter of feast, which worthily deserved noting.
MAECENAS: She's a most triumphant Lady, if report be square to her.
DOMITIUS: When she first met Mark Antony, she purs'd up his heart, upon the river of Cydnus.
AGRIPPA: There she appear'd indeed; or my reporter devis'd well for her.
DOMITIUS: I will tell you.
The barge she sat in, like a burnish'd throne,
Burn't on the water: the poop was beaten gold;

Purple the sails, and so perfumed that
The winds were love-sick with them; the oars were silver,
Which to the tune of flutes kept stroke, and made
The water which they beat to follow faster,
As amorous of their strokes. For her own person,
It beggar'd all description: she did lie
In her pavilion—cloth of gold, of tissue—
O'er-picturing that Venus, where we see
The fancy outwork nature: on each side her
Stood pretty dimpled boys, like smiling Cupids,
With divers-colour'd fans, whose wind did seem
To glow the delicate cheeks which they did cool,
And what they undid did.
AGRIPPA: O, rare for Antony!
DOMITIUS: Her gentlewomen, like the Nereides,
So many mermaids, tended her i' th' eyes,
And made their bends adornings: at the helm
A seeming mermaid steers: the silken tackle
Swell with the touches of those flower-soft hands,
That yarely frame the office. From the barge
A strange invisible perfume hits the sense
Of the adjacent wharfs. The city cast
Her people out upon her; and Antony,
Enthroned i' th' market-place, did sit alone,
Whistling to the air; which, but for vacancy,
Had gone to gaze on Cleopatra too,
And made a gap in Nature.
AGRIPPA: Rare Egyptian!
DOMITIUS: Upon her landing, Antony sent to her,
Invited her to supper: she replied,
It should be better he became her guest;
Which she entreated: our courteous Antony,
Whom ne'er the word of 'No' woman heard speak,
Being barber'd ten times o'er, goes to the feast,

And for his ordinary pays his heart,
For what his eyes eat only.
AGRIPPA: Royal wench!
She made great Caesar lay his sword to bed:
He plough'd her, and she cropp'd.
DOMITIUS: I saw her once
Hop forty paces through the public street;
And having lost her breath, she spoke, and panted,
That she did make defect, perfection,
And breathless, power breathe forth.
MAECENAS: Now Antony must leave her utterly.
DOMITIUS: Never; he will not:
Age cannot wither her, nor custom stale
Her infinite variety: other women cloy
The appetites they feed: but she makes hungry
Where most she satisfies; for vilest things
Become themselves in her: that the holy priests
Bless her when she is riggish.
MAECENAS: If beauty, wisdom, modesty, can settle
The heart of Antony, Octavia is
A blessed lottery to him.
AGRIPPA: Let us go.
Good Enobarbus, make yourself my guest
Whilst you abide here.
DOMITIUS: Humbly, sir, I thank you.
Exeunt.

II. 3

Enter Antony, Caesar, Octavia between them, and Attendants.

ANTONY: The world and my great office will sometimes Divide me from your bosom.
OCTAVIA: All which time
Before the gods my knee shall bow my prayers
To them for you.

ANTONY: Good night, sir. My Octavia,
Read not my blemishes in the world's report:
I have not kept my square; but that to come
Shall all be done by the rule. Good night, dear Lady.
Good night, sir.
CAESAR: Good night.
Exeunt Caesar and Octavia.
Enter Soothsayer.
ANTONY: Now, sirrah; you do wish yourself in Egypt?
Soothsayer: Would I had never come from thence, nor you thither!
ANTONY: If you can, your reason?
Soothsayer: I see it in
My motion, have it not in my tongue: but yet
Hie you to Egypt again.
ANTONY: Say to me,
Whose fortunes shall rise higher, Caesar's or mine?
Soothsayer: Caesar's.
Therefore, O Antony, stay not by his side:
Thy demon, that's thy spirit which keeps thee, is
Noble, courageous high, unmatchable,
Where Caesar's is not; but, near him, thy angel
Becomes a fear, as being o'erpower'd: therefore
Make space enough between you.
ANTONY: Speak this no more.
Soothsayer: To none but thee; no more, but when to thee.
If thou dost play with him at any game,
Thou art sure to lose; and, of that natural luck,
He beats thee 'gainst the odds: thy lustre thickens,
When he shines by: I say again, thy spirit
Is all afraid to govern thee near him;
But, he away, 'tis noble.
ANTONY: Get thee gone:
Say to Ventidius I would speak with him:

Exit Soothsayer.
He shall to Parthia. Be it art or hap,
He hath spoken true: the very dice obey him;
And in our sports my better cunning faints,
Under his chance: if we draw lots, he speeds;
His cocks do win the battle, still of mine,
When it is all to nought; and his quails ever
Beat mine, inhoop'd, at odds. I will to Egypt:
And though I make this marriage for my peace,
I' th' East my pleasure lies.
Enter Ventidius.
O, come, Ventidius,
You must to Parthia: your commission's ready;
Follow me, and receive't.

Exeunt.

II. 4

Enter Lepidus, Maecenas, and Agrippa.

LEPIDUS: Trouble yourselves no further: pray you, hasten
Your generals after.
AGRIPPA: Sir, Mark Antony
Will e'en but kiss Octavia, and we'll follow.
LEPIDUS: Till I shall see you in your soldier's dress,
Which will become you both, farewell.
MAECENAS: We shall,
As I conceive the journey, be at the Mount
Before you, Lepidus.
LEPIDUS: Your way is shorter;
My purposes do draw me much about:
You'll win two days upon me.
MAECENAS: Sir, good success!
LEPIDUS: Farewell.

Exeunt.

II. 5

Enter Cleopatra, Charmian, Iras and Alexas.

CLEOPATRA: Give me some music; music, moody food
Of us that trade in love.

Attendants: The music, ho!

Enter Mardian.

CLEOPATRA: Let it alone; let's to billiards: come, Charmian.

CHARMIAN: My arm is sore; best play with Mardian.

CLEOPATRA: As well a woman with an eunuch play'd
As with a woman. Come, you'll play with me, sir?

MARDIAN: As well as I can, Madam.

CLEOPATRA: And when good will is show'd,
Though't come too short,
The actor may plead pardon. I'll none now:
Give me mine angle; we'll to the river: there,
My music playing far off, I will betray
Tawny-finn'd fishes; my bended hook shall pierce
Their slimy jaws; and, as I draw them up,
I'll think them every one an Antony,
And say 'Ah, ha! you're caught.'

CHARMIAN: 'Twas merry when
You wager'd on your angling; when your diver
Did hang a salt-fish on his hook, which he
With fervency drew up.

CLEOPATRA: That time—O times!—
I laugh'd him out of patience; and that night
I laugh'd him into patience; and next morn,
Ere the ninth hour, I drunk him to his bed;
Then put my tires and mantles on him, whilst
I wore his sword Philippan,
O, from Italy
Enter a Messenger.
Ram thou thy fruitful tidings in mine ears,

That long time have been barren.
Messenger: Madam, Madam—
CLEOPATRA: Antoy is dead!—If thou say so, villain,
Thou kill'st thy Mistress: but well and free,
If thou so yield him, there is gold, and here
My bluest veins to kiss; a hand that kings
Have lipp'd, and trembled kissing.
Messenger: First, Madam, he is well.
CLEOPATRA: Why, there's more gold.
But, sirrah, mark, we use
To say the dead are well: bring it to that,
The gold I give thee will I melt and pour
Down thy ill-uttering throat.
Messenger: Good Madam, hear me.
CLEOPATRA: Well, go to, I will;
But there's no goodness in thy face: if Antony
Be free and healthful—so tart a favour
To trumpet such good tidings! If not well,
Thou shouldst come like a Fury crown'd with snakes,
Not like a formal man.
Messenger: Will't please you hear me?
CLEOPATRA: I have a mind to strike thee ere thou speak'st:
Yet if thou say Antony lives, is well,
Or friends with Caesar, or not captive to him,
I'll set thee in a shower of gold, and hail
Rich pearls upon thee.
Messenger: Madam, he's well.
CLEOPATRA: Well said.
Messenger: And friends with Caesar.
CLEOPATRA: Thou'rt an honest man.
Messenger: Caesar and he are greater friends than ever.
CLEOPATRA: Make thee a fortune from me.
Messenger: But yet, Madam—

CLEOPATRA: I do not like 'But yet,' it does allay
The good precedence; fie upon 'But yet'!
'But yet' is as a gaoler to bring forth
Some monstrous malefactor. Prithee, friend,
Pour out the pack of matter to mine ear,
The good and bad together: he's friends with Caesar:
In state of health thou say'st; and thou say'st, free.
Messenger: Free, Madam! no; I made no such report:
He's bound unto Octavia.
CLEOPATRA: For what good turn?
Messenger: For the best turn i' th' bed.
CLEOPATRA: I am pale, Charmian.
Messenger: Madam, he's married to Octavia.
CLEOPATRA: The most infectious pestilence upon thee!
Strikes him down.
Messenger: Good Madam, patience.
CLEOPATRA: What say you? Hence,
Strikes him again.
Horrible villain! or I'll spurn thine eyes
Like balls before me; I'll unhair thy head:
She hales him up and down.
Thou shalt be whipp'd with wire, and stew'd in brine,
Smarting in lingering pickle.
Messenger: Gracious Madam,
I that do bring the news, made not the match.
CLEOPATRA: Say 'tis not so, a province I will give thee,
And make thy fortunes proud: the blow thou hadst
Shall make thy peace for moving me to rage;
And I will boot thee with what gift beside
Thy modesty can beg.
Messenger: He's married, Madam.
CLEOPATRA: Rogue, thou hast liv'd too long.

Draws a knife.

Messenger: Nay, then I'll run.

What mean you, Madam? I have made no fault.

Exit.

CHARMIAN: Good Madam, keep yourself within yourself:

The man is innocent.

CLEOPATRA: Some innocents 'scape not the thunderbolt.

Melt Egypt into Nile! and kindly creatures
Turn all to serpents! Call the slave again:
Though I am mad, I will not bite him: call.

CHARMIAN: He is afeard to come.

CLEOPATRA: I will not hurt him.

Exit Charmian.

These hands do lack nobility, that they strike
A meaner than myself; since I myself
Have given myself the cause.

Enter Charmian and Messenger.

Come hither, sir.
Though it be honest, it is never good
To bring bad news: give to a gracious message.
An host of tongues; but let ill tidings tell
Themselves when they be felt.

Messenger: I have done my duty.

CLEOPATRA: Is he married?
I cannot hate thee worser than I do,
If thou again say 'Yes.'

Messenger: He's married, Madam.

CLEOPATRA: The gods confound thee! Dost thou hold there still?

Messenger: Should I lie, Madam?

CLEOPATRA: O, I would thou didst,
So half my Egypt were submerg'd and made
A cistern for scal'd snakes! Go, get thee hence:

Hadst thou Narcissus in thy face, to me
Thou wouldst appear most ugly. He is married?
Messenger: I crave your Highness' pardon.
CLEOPATRA: He is married?
Messenger: Take no offence that I would not offend you:
To punish me for what you make me do.
Seems much unequal: he's married to Octavia.
CLEOPATRA: O, that his fault should make a knave of thee,
That art not what thou'rt sure of! Get thee hence:
The merchandise which thou hast brought from Rome
Are all too dear for me: lie they upon thy hand,
And be undone by 'em!

Exit Messenger.

CHARMIAN: Good your Highness, patience.
CLEOPATRA: In praising Antony, I have dispraised Caesar.
CHARMIAN: Many times, Madam.
CLEOPATRA: I am paid for't now.
Lead me from hence:
I faint: O Iras, Charmian! 'tis no matter.
Go to the fellow, good Alexas; bid him
Report the feature of Octavia, her years,
Her inclination, let him not leave out
The colour of her hair: bring me word quickly.

Exit Alexas.

Let him for ever go: – let him not – Charmian,
Though he be painted one way like a Gorgon,
The other way's a Mars. Bid you Alexas
To Mardian.
Bring me word how tall she is. Pity me, Charmian,
But do not speak to me. Lead me to my chamber.

Exeunt.

II. 6

Flourish. Enter Pompey and Menas at one door, with drum and trumpet: at another, Caesar, Antony, Agrippa, Lepidus, Domitius, Maecenas, with Soldiers marching.

POMPEY: Your hostages I have, so have you mine;
And we shall talk before we fight.
CAESAR: Most meet
That first we come to words; and therefore have we
Our written purposes before us sent;
Which, if thou hast consider'd, let us know
If 'twill tie up thy discontented sword,
And carry back to Sicily much tall youth
That else must perish here.
POMPEY: To you all three,
The senators alone of this great world,
Chief factors for the gods, I do not know
Wherefore my father should revengers want,
Having a son and friends; since Julius Caesar,
Who at Philippi the good Brutus ghosted,
There saw you labouring for him. What was't
That mov'd pale Cassius to conspire; and what
Made the all-honour'd, honest Roman, Brutus,
With the arm'd rest, courtiers and beauteous freedom,
To drench the Capitol; but that they would
Have one man but a man? And that is it
Hath made me rig my navy; at whose burthen
The anger'd ocean foams; with which I meant
To scourge the ingratitude that despiteful Rome
Cast on my noble father.
CAESAR: Take your time.
ANTONY: Thou canst not fear us, Pompey, with thy sails;
We'll speak with thee at sea: at land, thou know'st

How much we do o'er-count thee.
POMPEY: At land, indeed,
Thou dost o'er-count me of my father's house:
But, since the cuckoo builds not for himself,
Remain in't as thou mayst.
LEPIDUS: Be pleas'd to tell us—
For this is from the present—how you take
The offers we have sent you.
CAESAR: There's the point.
ANTONY: Which do not be entreated to, but weigh
What it is worth embrac'd.
CAESAR: And what may follow,
To try a larger fortune.
POMPEY: You have made me offer
Of Sicily, Sardinia; and I must
Rid all the sea of pirates; then, to send
Measures of wheat to Rome; this 'greed upon
To part with unhack'd edges, and bear back
Our targes undinted.
all: That's our offer.
POMPEY: Know, then, I came before you here,
A man prepared
To take this offer: but Mark Antony
Put me to some impatience: though I lose
The praise of it by telling, you must know,
When Caesar and your brother were at blows,
Your mother came to Sicily and did find
Her welcome friendly.
ANTONY: I have heard it, Pompey;
And am well studied for a liberal thanks
Which I do owe you.
POMPEY: Let me have your hand:
I did not think, sir, to have met you here.
ANTONY: The beds i' th' East are soft; and thanks to
you,

That call'd me timelier than my purpose hither;
For I have gain'd by 't.
CAESAR: Since I saw you last,
There is a change upon you.
POMPEY: Well, I know not
What counts harsh fortune casts upon my face;
But in my bosom shall she never come,
To make my heart her vassal.
LEPIDUS: Well met here.
POMPEY: I hope so, Lepidus. Thus we are agreed:
I crave our composition may be written,
And seal'd between us.
CAESAR: That's the next to do.
POMPEY: We'll feast each other ere we part; and let's
Draw lots who shall begin.
ANTONY: That will I, Pompey.
POMPEY: No, Antony, take the lot: but, first
Or last, your fine Egyptian cookery
Shall have the fame. I have heard that Julius Caesar
Grew fat with feasting there.
ANTONY: You have heard much.
POMPEY: I have fair meanings, sir.
ANTONY: And fair words to them.
POMPEY: Then so much have I heard:
And I have heard, Apollodorus carried—
DOMITIUS: No more of that: he did so.
POMPEY: What, I pray you?
DOMITIUS: A certain Queen to Caesar in a mattress.
POMPEY: I know thee now: how farest thou, soldier?
DOMITIUS: Well;
And well am like to do; for, I perceive,
Four feasts are toward.
POMPEY: Let me shake thy hand;
I never hated thee: I have seen thee fight,
When I have envied thy behaviour.

DOMITIUS: Sir,
I never loved you much; but I ha' prais'd ye,
When you have well deserv'd ten times as much
As I have said you did.
POMPEY: Enjoy thy plainness,
It nothing ill becomes thee.
Aboard my galley I invite you all:
Will you lead, Lords? Show us the way, sir.
POMPEY: Come.

Exeunt all but Menas and Domitius.

MENAS: Thy father, Pompey, would ne'er have made this treaty—You and I have known, sir.

DOMITIUS: At sea, I think.

MENAS: We have, sir.

DOMITIUS: You have done well by water.

MENAS: And you by land.

DOMITIUS: I will praise any man that will praise me; though it cannot be denied what I have done by land.

MENAS: Nor what I have done by water.

DOMITIUS: Yes, something you can deny for your own safety: you have been a great thief by sea.

MENAS: And you by land.

DOMITIUS: There I deny my land service. But give me your hand, Menas: if our eyes had authority, here they might take two thieves kissing.

MENAS: All men's faces are true, whatsome'er their hands are.

DOMITIUS: But there is never a fair woman has a true face.

MENAS: No slander; they steal hearts.

DOMITIUS: We came hither to fight with you.

MENAS: For my part, I am sorry it is turn'd to a drinking.
Pompey doth this day laugh away his fortune.

DOMITIUS: If he do, sure, he cannot weep't back again.

MENAS: You've said, sir. We look'd not for Mark Antony here: pray you, is he married to Cleopatra?

DOMITIUS: Caesar's sister is called Octavia.

MENAS: True, sir; she was the wife of Caius Marcellus.

DOMITIUS: But she is now the wife of Marcus Antonius.

MENAS: Pray ye, sir?

DOMITIUS: 'Tis true.

MENAS: Then is Caesar and he for ever knit together.

DOMITIUS: If I were bound to divine of this unity, I would not prophesy so.

MENAS: I think the policy of that purpose made more in the marriage than the love of the parties.

DOMITIUS: I think so too. But you shall find the band that seems to tie their friendship together will be the very strangler of their amity: Octavia is of a holy, cold, and still conversation.

MENAS: Who would not have his wife so?

DOMITIUS: Not he that himself is not so; which is Mark Antony. He will to his Egyptian dish again: then shall the sighs of Octavia blow the fire up in Caesar; and, as I said before, that which is the strength of their amity, shall prove the immediate author of their variance. Antony will use his affection where it is: he married but his occasion here.

MENAS: And thus it may be. Come, sir, will you aboard?
I have a health for you.

DOMITIUS: I shall take it, sir: we have used our throats in Egypt.

MENAS: Come, let's away.

Exeunt.

II. 7

Music plays.

Enter two or three Servants with a banquet.

First Servant: Here they'll be, man. Some o' their plants are ill-rooted already: the least wind i' th' world will blow them down.

Second Servant: Lepidus is high-colour'd.

First Servant: They have made him drink alms-drink.

Second Servant: As they pinch one another by the disposition, he cries out 'No more;' reconciles them to his entreaty, and himself to the drink.

First Servant: But it raises the greater war between him and his discretion.

Second Servant: Why, this is to have a name in great men's fellowship: I had as lief have a reed that will do me no service, as a partisan I could not heave.

First Servant: To be called into a huge sphere, and not to be seen to move in't, are the holes where eyes should be, which pitifully disaster the cheeks.

A sennet sounded.

Enter Caesar, Antony, Lepidus, Pompey, Agrippa, Maecenas, Domitius, Menas, with other captains.

ANTONY: Thus do they, sir: they take the flow o' th' Nile
By certain scales i' the pyramid; they know,
By the height, th' lowness, or the mean, if dearth
Or foison follow: the higher Nilus swells,
The more it promises: as it ebbs, the seedsman
Upon the slime and ooze scatters his grain,
And shortly comes to harvest.

LEPIDUS: You've strange serpents there.

ANTONY: Ay, Lepidus.

LEPIDUS: Your serpent of Egypt is bred now of your mud by the operation of your sun: so is your crocodile.

ANTONY: They are so.

POMPEY: Sit—and some wine! A health to Lepidus!

LEPIDUS: I am not so well as I should be, but I'll ne'er out.

DOMITIUS: Not till you have slept; I fear me you'll be in till then.

LEPIDUS: Nay, certainly, I have heard the Ptolemies' pyramises are very goodly things; without contradiction, I have heard that.

MENAS: Pompey, a word.

POMPEY: Say in mine ear: what is't?

MENAS: Forsake thy seat, I do beseech thee, captain,
And hear me speak a word.

POMPEY: Forbear me till anon.
This wine for Lepidus!

LEPIDUS: What manner o' thing is your crocodile?

ANTONY: It is shaped, sir, like itself; and it is as broad as it hath breadth: it is just so high as it is, and moves with its own organs: it lives by that which nourisheth it; and the elements once out of it, it transmigrates.

LEPIDUS: What colour is it of?

ANTONY: Of it own colour too.

LEPIDUS: 'Tis a strange serpent.

ANTONY: 'Tis so. And the tears of it are wet.

CAESAR: Will this description satisfy him?

ANTONY: With the health that Pompey gives him, else he is a very epicure.

POMPEY: Go hang, sir, hang! Tell me of that? Away!
Do as I bid you. Where's this cup I call'd for?

MENAS: If for the sake of merit thou wilt hear me,
Rise from thy stool.

POMPEY: I think thou'rt mad.
The matter?
Rises, and walks aside.

MENAS: I have ever held my cap off to thy fortunes.
POMPEY: Thou hast serv'd me with much faith. What's else to say? Be jolly, Lords.
ANTONY: These quick-sands, Lepidus,
Keep off them, for you sink.
MENAS: Wilt thou be Lord of all the world?
POMPEY: What say'st thou?
MENAS: Wilt thou be Lord of the whole world? That's twice.
POMPEY: How should that be?
MENAS: But entertain it,
And, though thou think me poor, I am the man
Will give thee all the world.
POMPEY: Hast thou drunk well?
MENAS: Now, Pompey, I have kept me from the cup.
Thou art, if thou dar'st be, the earthly Jove:
Whate'er the ocean pales, or sky inclips,
Is thine, if thou wilt ha't.
POMPEY: Show me which way.
MENAS: These three world-sharers, these competitors,
Are in thy vessel: let me cut the cable;
And, when we are put off, fall to their throats:
All there is thine.
POMPEY: Ah, this thou shouldst have done,
And not have spoke on't! In me 'tis villainy;
In thee't had been good service. Thou must know,
'Tis not my profit that does lead mine honour;
Mine honour it. Repent that e'er thy tongue
Hath so betray'd thine act: being done unknown,
I should have found it afterwards well done;
But must condemn it now. Desist, and drink.
MENAS: For this,
I'll never follow thy pall'd fortunes more.
Who seeks, and will not take when once 'tis offer'd,
Shall never find it more.

POMPEY: This health to Lepidus!
ANTONY: Bear him ashore. I'll pledge it for him, Pompey.
DOMITIUS: Here's to thee, Menas!
MENAS: Enobarbus, welcome!
POMPEY: Fill till the cup be hid.
DOMITIUS: There's a strong fellow, Menas.
Pointing to the Attendant who carries off Lepidus.
MENAS: Why?
DOMITIUS: A' bears the third part of the world, man; see'st not?
MENAS: The third part, then, is drunk: would it were all,
That it might go on wheels!
DOMITIUS: Drink thou; increase the reels.
MENAS: Come.
POMPEY: This is not yet an Alexandrian feast.
ANTONY: It ripens towards it. Strike the vessels, ho?
Here is to Caesar!
CAESAR: I could well forbear't.
It's monstrous labour, when I wash my brain,
And it grows fouler.
ANTONY: Be a child o' th' time.
CAESAR: Possess it, I'll make answer:
But I had rather fast from all four days
Than drink so much in one.
DOMITIUS: Ha, my brave Emperor!
Shall we dance now the Egyptian Bacchanals,
And celebrate our drink?
POMPEY: Let's ha't, good soldier.
ANTONY: Come, let's all take hands,
Till that the conquering wine hath steep'd our sense
In soft and delicate Lethe.
DOMITIUS: All take hands.
Make battery to our ears with the loud music:

The while, I'll place you: then the boy shall sing;
The holding every man shall bear 't as loud
As his strong sides can volley.
Music plays. Domitius places them hand in hand.

THE SONG

Come, thou Monarch of the Vine,
Plumpy Bacchus with pink eyne!
In thy fats our cares be drown'd,
With thy grapes our hairs be crown'd:
Cup us, till the world go round,
Cup us, till the world go round!

CAESAR: What would you more?
Pompey, good night. Good brother,
Let me request you off: our graver business
Frowns at this levity. Gentle Lords, let's part;
You see we have burnt our cheeks: strong Enobarb
Is weaker than the wine; and mine own tongue
Splits what it speaks: the wild disguise hath almost
Antick'd us all. What needs more words? Good night.
Good Antony, your hand.
POMPEY: I'll try you on the shore.
ANTONY: And shall, sir; give's your hand.
POMPEY: O Antony,
You have my father's house—But, what, we are friends.
Come, down into the boat.
DOMITIUS: Take heed you fall not.
Menas, I'll not on shore.
Exeunt all but Domitius and Menas.
MENAS: No, to my cabin.
These drums! these trumpets, flutes! what!
Let Neptune hear we bid a loud farewell
To these great fellows: sound and be hang'd, sound

out!

Sound a flourish with drums.

DOMITIUS: Ho! says a' there's my cap.

MENAS: Ho! Noble captain, come.

Exeunt.

III. 1

Enter Ventidius as it were in triumph, with Silius and other Roman Officers and Soldiers; the dead body of Pacorus borne before him.

VENTIDIUS: Now, darting Parthia, art thou struck; and now
Pleased fortune does of Marcus Crassus' death
Make me revenger. Bear the King's son's body
Before our army. Thy Pacorus, Orodes,
Pays this for Marcus Crassus.

SILIUS: Noble Ventidius,
Whilst yet with Parthian blood thy sword is warm,
The fugitive Parthians follow; spur through Media,
Mesopotamia, and the shelters, whither
The routed fly: so thy grand captain Antony
Shall set thee on triumphant chariots and
Put garlands on thy head.

VENTIDIUS: O Silius, Silius,
I have done enough; a lower place, note well,
May make too great an act: for learn this, Silius;
Better to leave undone, than by our deed
Acquire too high a fame when him we serve's away.
Caesar and Antony have ever won
More in their officer than person: Sossius,
One of my place in Syria, his lieutenant,
For quick accumulation of renown,
Which he achiev'd by the minute, lost his favour.
Who does i' th' wars more than his captain can
Becomes his captain's captain: and ambition,

The soldier's virtue, rather makes choice of loss,
Than gain, which darkens him.
I could do more to do Antonius good,
But 'twould offend him; and in his offence
Should my performance perish.

SILIUS: Thou hast, Ventidius, that
Without the which a soldier and his sword,
Grants scarce distinction. Thou wilt write to Antony!

VENTIDIUS: I'll humbly signify what in his name,
That magical word of war, we have effected;
How, with his banners and his well-paid ranks,
The ne'er-yet-beaten horse of Parthia
We have jaded out o' th' field.

SILIUS: Where is he now?

VENTIDIUS: He purposeth to Athens: whither, with what haste
The weight we must convey with's, will permit,
We shall appear before him. On there; pass along!

Exeunt.

III. 2

Enter Agrippa at one door, Domitius at another.

AGRIPPA: What, are the brothers parted?

DOMITIUS: They have dispatch'd with Pompey, he is gone;
The other three are sealing. Octavia weeps
To part from Rome; Caesar is sad; and Lepidus,
Since Pompey's feast, as Menas says, is troubled
With the green sickness.

AGRIPPA: 'Tis a noble Lepidus.

DOMITIUS: A very fine one: O, how he loves Caesar!

AGRIPPA: Nay, but how dearly he adores Mark Antony!

DOMITIUS: Caesar? Why, he's the Jupiter of men.

AGRIPPA: What's Antony? The god of Jupiter.

DOMITIUS: Spake you of Caesar? How! the non-pareil!
AGRIPPA: O Antony! O thou Arabian bird!
DOMITIUS: Would you praise Caesar, say 'Caesar:' go no further.
AGRIPPA: Indeed, he plied them both with excellent praises.
DOMITIUS: But he loves Caesar best; yet he loves Antony: Ho! hearts, tongues, figures, scribes, bards, poets, cannot
Think, speak, cast, write, sing, number, ho!
His love to Antony. But as for Caesar,
Kneel down, kneel down, and wonder.
AGRIPPA: Both he loves.
DOMITIUS: They are his shards, and he their beetle. So;
This is to horse. Adieu, noble Agrippa.
AGRIPPA: Good fortune, worthy soldier; and farewell.
Enter Caesar, Antony, Lepidus and Octavia.
ANTONY: No further, sir.
CAESAR: You take from me a great part of myself;
Use me well in, 't. Sister, prove such a wife
As my thoughts make thee, and as my farthest band
Shall pass on thy approof. Most noble Antony,
Let not the piece of virtue, which is set
Betwixt us, as the cement of our love,
To keep it builded, be the ram to batter
The fortress of it; for better might we
Have lov'd without this mean, if on both parts
This be not cherish'd.
ANTONY: Make me not offended
In your distrust.
CAESAR: I have said.
ANTONY: You shall not find,
Though you be therein curious, the least cause
For what you seem to fear: so, the gods keep you,

And make the hearts of Romans serve your ends!
We will here part.
CAESAR: Farewell, my dearest sister, fare thee well:
The elements be kind to thee, and make
Thy spirits all of comfort! fare thee well.
OCTAVIA: My noble brother!
ANTONY: The April 's in her eyes: it is love's spring,
And these the showers to bring it on. Be cheerful.
OCTAVIA: Sir, look well to my husband's house; and–
CAESAR: What, Octavia?
OCTAVIA: I'll tell you in your ear.
ANTONY: Her tongue will not obey her heart, nor can
Her heart inform her tongue–the swan's down-feather,
That stands upon the swell at full of tide,
And neither way inclines.
DOMITIUS: Will Caesar weep?
AGRIPPA: He has a cloud in 's face.
DOMITIUS: He were the worse for that, were he a horse;
So is he, being a man.
AGRIPPA: Why, Enobarbus,
When Antony found Julius Caesar dead,
He cried almost to roaring; and he wept
When at Philippi he found Brutus slain.
DOMITIUS: That year, indeed, he was troubled with a rheum;
What willingly he did confound he wail'd,
Believe't, till I weep too.
CAESAR: No, sweet Octavia,
You shall hear from me still; the time shall not
Out-go my thinking on you.
ANTONY: Come, sir, come;
I'll wrastle with you in my strength of love:

Look, here I have you; thus I let you go,
And give you to the gods.
CAESAR: Adieu; be happy!
LEPIDUS: Let all the number of the stars give light
To thy fair way!
CAESAR: Farewell, farewell!
ANTONY: Farewell!

Trumpets sound.
Exeunt.

III. 3

Enter Cleopatra, Charmian, Iras and Alexas.

CLEOPATRA: Where is the fellow?
ALEXAS: Half afeard to come.
CLEOPATRA: Go to, go to.

Enter the Messenger as before.

Come hither, sir.
ALEXAS: Good majesty,
Herod of Jewry dare not look upon you
But when you are well pleased.
CLEOPATRA: That Herod's head
I'll have: but how, when Antony is gone
Through whom I might command it? Come thou near.
Messenger: Most gracious Majesty—
CLEOPATRA: Didst thou behold Octavia?
Messenger: Ay, dread Queen.
CLEOPATRA: Where?
Messenger: Madam, in Rome;
I look'd her in the face, and saw her led
Between her brother and Mark Antony.
CLEOPATRA: Is she as tall as me?
Messenger: She is not, Madam.
CLEOPATRA: Didst hear her speak? Is she shrill-tongued or low?

Messenger: Madam, I heard her speak; she is low-voiced.

CLEOPATRA: That's not so good: he cannot like her long.

CHARMIAN: Like her! O Isis! 'tis impossible.

CLEOPATRA: I think so, Charmian: dull of tongue, and dwarfish!
What majesty is in her gait? Remember,
If e'er thou look'dst on majesty.

Messenger: She creeps:
Her motion and her station are as one;
She shows a body rather than a life,
A statue than a breather.

CLEOPATRA: Is this certain?

Messenger: Or I have no observance.

CHARMIAN: Three in Egypt
Cannot make better note.

CLEOPATRA: He's very knowing;
I do perceive't: there's nothing in her yet:
The fellow has good judgment.

CHARMIAN: Excellent.

CLEOPATRA: Guess at her years, I prithee.

Messenger: Madam,
She was a widow—

CLEOPATRA: Widow! Charmian, hark.

Messenger: And I do think she's thirty.

CLEOPATRA: Bear'st thou her face in mind? is't long or round?

Messenger: Round even to faultiness.

CLEOPATRA: For the most part, too, they are foolish that are so.
Her hair, what colour?

Messenger: Brown, Madam: and her forehead
As low as she would wish it.

CLEOPATRA: There's gold for thee.

Thou must not take my former sharpness ill:
I will employ thee back again; I find thee
Most fit for business: go make thee ready;
Our letters are prepared.

Exit Messenger.

CHARMIAN: A proper man.

CLEOPATRA: Indeed, he is so: I repent me much
That so I harried him. Why, methinks, by him,
This creature's no such thing.

CHARMIAN: Nothing, Madam.

CLEOPATRA: The man hath seen some Majesty, and should know.

CHARMIAN: Hath he seen Majesty? Isis else defend,
And serving you so long!

CLEOPATRA: I have one thing more to ask him yet, good Charmian:
But 'tis no matter; thou shalt bring him to me
Where I will write. All may be well enough.

CHARMIAN: I warrant you, Madam.

Exeunt.

III. 4

Enter Antony and Octavia.

ANTONY: Nay, nay, Octavia, not only that—
That were excusable, that, and thousands more
Of semblable import—but he hath wag'd
New wars 'gainst Pompey; made his will, and read it
To public ear:
Spoke scantly of me: when perforce he could not
But pay me terms of honour, cold and sickly
He vented them; most narrow measure lent me:
When the best hint was given him, he not took't,
Or did it from his teeth.

OCTAVIA: O my good Lord,

Believe not all; or, if you must believe,
Stomach not all. A more unhappy lady,
If this division chance, ne'er stood between,
Praying for both parts:
The good gods will mock me presently,
When I shall pray, 'O bless my Lord and husband!'
Undo that prayer, by crying out as loud,
'O, bless my brother!' Husband win, win brother,
Prays, and destroys the prayer; no midway
'Twixt these extremes at all.
ANTONY: Gentle Octavia,
Let your best love draw to that point, which seeks
Best to preserve it: if I lose mine honour,
I lose myself: better I were not yours
Than yours so branchless. But, as you requested,
Yourself shall go between 's: the mean time, Lady,
I'll raise the preparation of a war
Shall stain your brother: make your soonest haste;
So your desires are yours.
OCTAVIA: Thanks to my Lord.
The Jove of power make me most weak, most weak,
Your reconciler! Wars 'twixt you twain would be,
As if the world should cleave, and that slain men
Should solder up the rift.
ANTONY: When it appears to you where this begins,
Turn your displeasure that way: for our faults
Can never be so equal, that your love
Can equally move with them. Provide your going;
Choose your own company, and command what cost
Your heart has mind to.

Exeunt.

III. 5

Enter Domitius and Eros.

DOMITIUS: How now, friend Eros!

EROS: There's strange news come, sir.

DOMITIUS: What, man?

EROS: Caesar and Lepidus have made wars upon Pompey.

DOMITIUS: This is old: what is the success?

EROS: Caesar, having made use of him in the wars 'gainst Pompey, presently denied him rivality; would not let him partake in the glory of the action: and not resting here, accuses him of letters he had formerly wrote to Pompey; upon his own appeal, seizes him: so the poor third is up, till death enlarge his confine.

DOMITIUS: Then, world, thou hast a pair of chaps, no more;
And throw between them all the food thou hast,
They'll grind the one the other. Where's Antony?

EROS: He's walking in the garden—thus; and spurns
The rush that lies before him; cries, 'Fool Lepidus!'
And threats the throat of that his officer
That murder'd Pompey.

DOMITIUS: Our great navy's rigg'd.

EROS: For Italy and Caesar. More, Domitius;
My Lord desires you presently: my news
I might have told hereafter.

DOMITIUS: 'Twill be naught:
But let it be. Bring me to Antony.

EROS: Come, sir.

Exeunt.

III. 6

Enter Caesar, Agrippa and Maecenas.

CAESAR: Contemning Rome, he has done all this, and

more,
In Alexandria: here's the manner of 't:
I' th' market-place, on a tribunal silver'd,
Cleopatra and himself in chairs of gold
Were publicly enthron'd: at the feet, sat
Caesarion, whom they call my father's son,
And all the unlawful issue that their lust
Since then hath made between them. Unto her
He gave the stablishment of Egypt; made her
Of lower Syria, Cyprus, Lydia,
Absolute Queen.
MAECENAS: This in the public eye?
CAESAR: I' th' common show-place, where they exercise.
His sons he there proclaim'd the Kings of kings:
Great Media, Parthia, and Armenia.
He gave to Alexander; to Ptolemy he assign'd
Syria, Cilicia, and Phoenicia: she
In the habiliments of the Goddess Isis
That day appear'd; and oft before gave audience,
As 'tis reported, so.
MAECENAS: Let Rome be thus inform'd.
AGRIPPA: Who, queasy with his insolence
Already, will their good thoughts call from him.
CAESAR: The people know it; and have now received
His accusations.
AGRIPPA: Who does he accuse?
CAESAR: Caesar: and that, having in Sicily
Sextus Pompeius spoil'd, we had not rated him
His part o' th' isle: then does he say, he lent me
Some shipping unrestor'd: lastly, he frets
That Lepidus of the triumvirate
Should be depos'd; and, being that, we detain
All his revenue.
AGRIPPA: Sir, this should be answer'd.

CAESAR: 'Tis done already, and the messenger gone.
I have told him, Lepidus was grown too cruel;
That he his high authority abused,
And did deserve his change: for what I have conquer'd,
I grant him part; but then, in his Armenia,
And other of his conquer'd kingdoms, I
Demand the like.

MAECENAS: He'll never yield to that.

CAESAR: Nor must not then be yielded to in this.

Enter Octavia with her train.

OCTAVIA: Hail, Caesar, and my lord! hail, most dear Caesar!

CAESAR: That ever I should call thee castaway!

OCTAVIA: You have not call'd me so, nor have you cause.

CAESAR: Why have you stol'n upon us thus! You come not
Like Caesar's sister: the wife of Antony
Should have an army for an usher, and
The neighs of horse to tell of her approach,
Long ere she did appear; the trees by the way
Should have borne men; and expectation fainted,
Longing for what it had not; nay, the dust
Should have ascended to the roof of heaven,
Rais'd by your populous troops: but you are come
A market-maid to Rome; and have prevented
The ostentation of our love, which, left unshown,
Is often left unlov'd; we should have met you
By sea and land; supplying every stage
With an augmented greeting.

OCTAVIA: Good my Lord,
To come thus was I not constrain'd, but did it
On my free will. My Lord, Mark Antony,
Hearing that you prepar'd for war, acquainted

My grieved ear withal; whereon, I begg'd
His pardon for return.
CAESAR: Which soon he granted,
Being an obstruct 'tween his lust and him.
OCTAVIA: Do not say so, my Lord.
CAESAR: I have eyes upon him,
And his affairs come to me on the wind.
Where is he now?
OCTAVIA: My Lord, in Athens.
CAESAR: No, my most wronged sister; Cleopatra
Hath nodded him to her. He hath given his empire
Up to a whore; who now are levying
The Kings o' th' earth for war; he hath assembled
Bocchus, the king of Libya; Archelaus,
Of Cappadocia; Philadelphos, King
Of Paphlagonia; the Thracian king, Adallas;
King Malchus of Arabia; King of Pont;
Herod of Jewry; Mithridates, King
Of Comagene; Polemon and Amyntas,
The Kings of Mede and Lycaonia,
With a more larger list of sceptres.
OCTAVIA: Ay me, most wretched,
That have my heart parted betwixt two friends
That do afflict each other!
CAESAR: Welcome hither:
Your letters did withhold our breaking forth;
Till we perceiv'd, both how you were wrong led,
And we in negligent danger. Cheer your heart;
Be you not troubled with the time, which drives
O'er your content these strong necessities;
But let determin'd things to destiny
Hold unbewail'd their way. Welcome to Rome;
Nothing more dear to me. You are abus'd
Beyond the mark of thought: and the high gods,
To do you justice, make them ministers

Of us and those that love you. Best of comfort;
And ever welcome to us.
AGRIPPA: Welcome, Lady.
MAECENAS: Welcome, dear Madam.
Each heart in Rome does love and pity you:
Only the adulterous Antony, most large
In his abominations, turns you off;
And gives his potent regiment to a trull,
That noises it against us.
OCTAVIA: Is it so, sir?
CAESAR: Most certain. Sister, welcome: pray you,
Be ever known to patience: my dear'st sister!
Exeunt.

III. 7

Enter Cleopatra and Domitius.

CLEOPATRA: I will be even with thee, doubt it not.
DOMITIUS: But why, why, why?
CLEOPATRA: Thou hast forspoke my being in these wars,
And say'st it is not fit.
DOMITIUS: Well, is it, is it?
CLEOPATRA: If not, denounced against us, why should not we
Be there in person?
DOMITIUS: Well, I could reply:
If we should serve with horse and mares together,
The horse were merely lost; the mares would bear
A soldier and his horse.
CLEOPATRA: What is't you say?
DOMITIUS: Your presence needs must puzzle Antony;
Take from his heart, take from his brain, from's time,
What should not then be spar'd. He is already
Traduc'd for levity; and 'tis said in Rome
That Photinus an eunuch and your maids

Manage this war.
CLEOPATRA: Sink Rome, and their tongues rot
That speak against us! A charge we bear i' th' war,
And, as the president of my kingdom, will
Appear there for a man. Speak not against it:
I will not stay behind.
DOMITIUS Nay, I have done.
Here comes the Emperor.
Enter Antony and Canidius.
ANTONY: Is it not strange, Canidius,
That from Tarentum and Brundusium
He could so quickly cut the Ionian sea,
And take in Toryne? You have heard on't, sweet?
CLEOPATRA: Celerity is never more admir'd
Than by the negligent.
ANTONY: A good rebuke,
Which might have well becomed the best of men,
To taunt at slackness. Canidius, we
Will fight with him by sea.
CLEOPATRA: By sea! what else?
CANIDIUS: Why will my Lord do so?
ANTONY: For that he dares us to't.
DOMITIUS: So hath my Lord dar'd him to single fight.
CANIDIUS: Ay, and to wage this battle at Pharsalia.
Where Caesar fought with Pompey: but these offers,
Which serve not for his vantage, be shakes off;
And so should you.
DOMITIUS: Your ships are not well mann'd;
Your mariners are muleters, reapers, people
Ingross'd by swift impress; in Caesar's fleet
Are those that often have 'gainst Pompey fought:
Their ships are yare; yours, heavy: no disgrace
Shall fall you for refusing him at sea,
Being prepar'd for land.
ANTONY: By sea, by sea.

DOMITIUS: Most worthy sir, you therein throw away
The absolute soldiership you have by land;
Distract your army, which doth most consist
Of war-mark'd footmen; leave unexecuted
Your own renowned knowledge; quite forego
The way which promises assurance; and
Give up yourself merely to chance and hazard,
From firm security.
ANTONY: I'll fight at sea.
CLEOPATRA: I have sixty sails, Caesar none better.
ANTONY: Our overplus of shipping will we burn;
And, with the rest full-mann'd, from the head of Actium
Beat the approaching Caesar. But if we fail,
We then can do't at land.
Enter a Messenger.
Thy business?
Messenger: The news is true, my Lord; he is descried;
Caesar has taken Toryne.
ANTONY: Can he be there in person? 'Tis impossible;
Strange that power should be. Canidius,
Our nineteen Legions thou shalt hold by land,
And our twelve thousand horse. We'll to our ship:
Away, my Thetis!
Enter a Soldier.
How now, worthy soldier?
Soldier: O noble Emperor, do not fight by sea;
Trust not to rotten planks: do you misdoubt
This sword and these my wounds? Let th' Egyptians
And the Phoenicians go a-ducking; we
Have us'd to conquer, standing on the earth,
And fighting foot to foot.
ANTONY: Well, well: away!
Exeunt Antony, Cleopatra and Domitius.
Soldier: By Hercules, I think I am i' th' right.

CANIDIUS: Soldier, thou art: but his whole action grows
Not in the power on't: so our leader's led,
And we are women's men.
Soldier: You keep by land
The legions and the horse whole, do you not?
CANIDIUS: Marcus Octavius, Marcus Justeius,
Publicola, and Caelius, are for sea:
But we keep whole by land. This speed of Caesar's
Carries beyond belief.
Soldier: While he was yet in Rome,
His power went out in such distractions as
Beguil'd all spies.
CANIDIUS: Who's his lieutenant, hear you?
Soldier: They say, one Taurus.
CANIDIUS: Well I know the man.

Enter a Messenger.

Messenger: The Emperor calls Canidius.
CANIDIUS: With news the time's with labour, and throes forth,
Each minute, some.

Exeunt.

III. 8

Enter Caesar and Taurus, with his army, marching.

CAESAR: Taurus!
TAURUS: My Lord?
CAESAR: Strike not by land; keep whole: provoke not battle,
Till we have done at sea. Do not exceed
The prescript of this scroll: our fortune lies
Upon this jump.

Exeunt.

III. 9

Enter Antony and Domitius.

ANTONY: Set we our squadrons on yond side o' th' hill,
In eye of Caesar's battle; from which place
We may the number of the ships behold,
And so proceed accordingly.

Exeunt.

III. 10

Canidius marcheth with his land army one way over the stage; and Taurus, the lieutenant of Caesar, the other way. After their going in, is heard the noise of a sea-fight Alarum. Enter Domitius.

DOMITIUS: Naught, naught all, naught! I can behold no longer:
The Antoniad, the Egyptian admiral,
With all their sixty, fly and turn the rudder:
To see't mine eyes are blasted.

Enter Scarus.

SCARUS: Gods and goddesses,
All the whole synod of them!

DOMITIUS: What's thy passion!

SCARUS: The greater cantle of the world is lost
With very ignorance; we have kiss'd away
Kingdoms and provinces.

DOMITIUS: How appears the fight?

SCARUS: On our side like the token'd pestilence,
Where death is sure. Yon ribaudred nag of Egypt—
Whom leprosy o'ertake!—i' th' midst o' th' fight,
When vantage like a pair of twins appear'd,
Both as the same, or rather ours the elder,
The breeze upon her, like a cow in June,
Hoists sails and flies.

DOMITIUS: That I beheld:

Mine eyes did sicken at the sight, and could not
Endure a further view.
SCARUS: She once being loof'd,
The noble ruin of her magic, Antony,
Claps on his sea-wing, and, like a doting mallard,
Leaving the fight in height, flies after her:
I never saw an action of such shame;
Experience, manhood, honour, ne'er before
Did violate so itself.
DOMITIUS: Alack, alack!

Enter Canidius.

CANIDIUS: Our fortune on the sea is out of breath,
And sinks most lamentably. Had our General
Been what he knew himself, it had gone well:
O, he has given example for our flight,
Most grossly, by his own!
DOMITIUS: Ay, are you thereabouts?
Why, then, good night indeed.
CANIDIUS: Toward Peloponnesus are they fled.
SCARUS: 'Tis easy to't; and there I will attend
What further comes.
CANIDIUS: To Caesar will I render
My legions and my horse: six Kings already
Show me the way of yielding.
DOMITIUS: I'll yet follow
The wounded chance of Antony, though my reason
Sits in the wind against me.

Exeunt.

III. 11

Enter Antony with Attendants.

ANTONY: Hark! the land bids me tread no more upon't;
It is ashamed to bear me! Friends, come hither:
I am so lated in the world, that I

Have lost my way for ever: I have a ship
Laden with gold; take that, divide it; fly,
And make your peace with Caesar.
All: Fly! not we.
ANTONY: I have fled myself; and have instructed cowards
To run and show their shoulders. Friends, be gone;
I have myself resolv'd upon a course
Which has no need of you; be gone:
My treasure's in the harbour, take it. O,
I follow'd that I blush to look upon:
My very hairs do mutiny; for the white
Reprove the brown for rashness, and they them
For fear and doting. Friends, be gone: you shall
Have letters from me to some friends that will
Sweep your way for you. Pray you, look not sad,
Nor make replies of loathness: take the hint
Which my despair proclaims; let that be left
Which leaves itself: to the sea-side straightway:
I will possess you of that ship and treasure.
Leave me, I pray, a little: pray you now:
Nay, do so; for, indeed, I have lost command,
Therefore I pray you: I'll see you by and by.
Enter Cleopatra led by Charmian, Iras and Eros.
EROS: Nay, gentle Madam, to him, comfort him.
IRAS: Do, most dear Queen.
CHARMIAN: Do! why: what else?
CLEOPATRA: Let me sit down. O Juno!
ANTONY: No, no, no, no, no.
EROS: See you here, sir?
ANTONY: O fie, fie, fie!
CHARMIAN: Madam!
IRAS: Madam, O good Empress!
EROS: Sir, sir—
ANTONY: Yes, my Lord, yes; he at Philippi kept

His sword e'en like a dancer; while I struck
The lean and wrinkled Cassius; and 'twas I
That the mad Brutus ended: he alone
Dealt on lieutenantry, and no practice had
In the brave squares of war: yet now—No matter.
CLEOPATRA: Ah, stand by.
EROS: The Queen, my Lord, the Queen.
IRAS: Go to him, madam, speak to him:
He is unqualitied with very shame.
CLEOPATRA: Well then, sustain him: O!
EROS: Most noble sir, arise; the Queen approaches:
Her head's declin'd, and death will seize her, but
Your comfort makes the rescue.
ANTONY: I have offended reputation,
A most unnoble swerving.
EROS: Sir, the Queen.
ANTONY: O, whither hast thou led me, Egypt? See,
How I convey my shame out of thine eyes
By looking back what I have left behind
'Stroy'd in dishonour.
CLEOPATRA: O my Lord, my Lord,
Forgive my fearful sails! I little thought
You would have follow'd.
ANTONY: Egypt, thou knew'st too well
My heart was to thy rudder tied by the strings,
And thou should'st stow me after: o'er my spirit
Thy full supremacy thou knew'st, and that
Thy beck, might from the bidding of the gods
Command me.
CLEOPATRA: O, my pardon!
ANTONY: Now I must
To the young man send humble treaties, dodge
And palter in the shifts of lowness; who
With half the bulk o' th' world play'd as I pleas'd,
Making and marring fortunes. You did know

How much you were my conqueror; and that
My sword, made weak by my affection, would
Obey it on all cause.
CLEOPATRA: Pardon, pardon!
ANTONY: Fall not a tear, I say; one of them rates
All that is won and lost: give me a kiss;
Even this repays me. We sent our schoolmaster;
Is he come back? Love, I am full of lead.
Some wine, within there, and our viands! Fortune knows
We scorn her most, when most she offers blows.
Exeunt.

III. 12

Enter Caesar, Dolabella, Thidias, with others.
CAESAR: Let him appear that's come from Antony.
Know you him?
DOLABELLA: Caesar, 'tis his schoolmaster:
An argument that he is pluck'd, when hither
He sends so poor a pinion off his wing,
Which had superfluous kings for messengers
Not many moons gone by.
Enter Euphronius, ambassador from Antony.
CAESAR: Approach, and speak.
EUPHRONIUS: Such as I am, I come from Antony:
I was of late as petty to his ends
As is the morn-dew on the myrtle-leaf
To his grand sea.
CAESAR: Be't so: declare thine office.
EUPHRONIUS: Lord of his fortunes, he salutes thee, and
Requires to live in Egypt: which not granted,
He lessens his requests; and to thee sues
To let him breathe between the heavens and earth,
A private man in Athens: this for him.

Next, Cleopatra does confess thy greatness;
Submits her to thy might; and of thee craves
The circle of the Ptolemies for her heirs,
Now hazarded to thy grace.
CAESAR: For Antony,
I have no ears to his request. The Queen
Of audience nor desire shall fail, so she
From Egypt drive her all-disgraced friend,
Or take his life there: this if she perform,
She shall not sue unheard. So to them both.
EUPHRONIUS: Fortune pursue thee!
CAESAR: Bring him through the bands.
Exit Euphronius.
From Antony win Cleopatra: promise,
And in our name, what she requires; add more,
From thine invention, offers: women are not
In their best fortunes strong; but want will perjure
The ne'er touch'd vestal: try thy cunning, Thidias;
Make thine own edict for thy pains, which we
Will answer as a law.
THIDIAS: Caesar, I go.
CAESAR: Observe how Antony becomes his flaw,
And what thou think'st his very action speaks
In every power that moves.
THIDIAS: Caesar, I shall.
Exeunt.

III. 13

Enter Cleopatra, Domitius, Charmian and Iras.
CLEOPATRA: What shall we do, Enobarbus?
DOMITIUS: Think, and die.
CLEOPATRA: Is Antony or we in fault for this?
DOMITIUS: Antony only, that would make his will
Lord of his reason. What though you fled
From that great face of war, whose several ranges

Frighted each other? Why should he follow?
The itch of his affection should not then
Have nick'd his captainship; at such a point,
When half to half the world oppos'd, he being
The meered question: 'twas a shame no less
Than was his loss, to course your flying flags,
And leave his navy gazing.
CLEOPATRA: Prithee, peace.
Enter Antony with Euphronius.
ANTONY: Is that his answer?
EUPHRONIUS: Ay, my Lord.
ANTONY: The Queen shall then have courtesy, so she
Will yield us up.
EUPHRONIUS: He says so.
ANTONY: Let her know't.
To the boy Caesar send this grizzled head,
And he will fill thy wishes to the brim
With Principalities.
CLEOPATRA: That head, my Lord?
ANTONY: To him again: tell him he wears the rose
Of youth upon him; from which the world should note
Something particular: his coin, ships, legions,
May be a coward's; whose ministers would prevail
Under the service of a child as soon
As i' th' command of Caesar: I dare him therefore
To lay his gay comparisons apart,
And answer me declin'd, sword against sword,
Ourselves alone. I'll write it: follow me.
Exeunt Antony and Euphronius.
DOMITIUS: Yes, like enough, high-battl'd Caesar will
Unstate his happiness, and be stag'd to the show,
Against a sworder! I see men's judgments are
A parcel of their fortunes; and things outward
Do draw the inward quality after them,

To suffer all alike. That he should dream,
Knowing all measures, the full Caesar will
Answer his emptiness! Caesar, thou hast subdued
His judgment too.

Enter an Attendant.

Attendant: A messenger from Caesar.

CLEOPATRA: What, no more ceremony? See, my women!
Against the blown rose may they stop their nose
That kneel'd unto the buds. Admit him, sir.

Exit Attendant.

DOMITIUS: Mine honesty and I begin to square.
The loyalty well held to fools, does make
Our faith mere folly: yet he that can endure
To follow with allegiance a fall'n Lord
Does conquer him that did his Master conquer
And earns a place i' th' story.

Enter Thidias.

CLEOPATRA: Caesar's will?

THIDIAS: Hear it apart.

CLEOPATRA: None but friends: say boldly.

THIDIAS: So, haply, are they friends to Antony.

DOMITIUS: He needs as many, sir, as Caesar has;
Or needs not us. If Caesar please, our Master
Will leap to be his friend: for us, you know,
Whose he is, we are, and that is, Caesar's.

THIDIAS: So.
Thus then, thou most renown'd: Caesar entreats,
Not to consider in what case thou stand'st,
Further than he is Caesar.

CLEOPATRA: Go on: right royal.

THIDIAS: He knows that you embrace not Antony
As you did love, but as you fear'd him.

CLEOPATRA: Oh!

THIDIAS: The scars upon your honour, therefore, he

Does pity, as constrained blemishes,
Not as deserved.
CLEOPATRA: He is a god, and knows
What is most right: mine honour was not yielded,
But conquer'd merely.
DOMITIUS: To be sure of that,
I will ask Antony. Sir, sir, thou art so leaky,
That we must leave thee to thy sinking, for
Thy dearest quit thee.

Exit.

THIDIAS: Shall I say to Caesar
What you require of him? for he partly begs
To be desired to give. It much would please him,
That of his fortunes you should make a staff
To lean upon: but it would warm his spirits,
To hear from me, you had left Antony,
And put yourself under his shrowd,
The universal landlord.
CLEOPATRA: What's your name?
THIDIAS: My name is Thidias.
CLEOPATRA: Most kind messenger,
Say to great Caesar this: in deputation
I kiss his conquering hand: tell him, I am prompt
To lay my crown at 's feet, and there to kneel:
Tell him from his all-obeying breath, I hear
The doom of Egypt.
THIDIAS: 'Tis your noblest course.
Wisdom and fortune combating together,
If that the former dare but what it can,
No chance may shake it. Give me grace to lay
My duty on your hand.
CLEOPATRA: Your Caesar's father oft,
When he hath mused of taking kingdoms in,
Bestow'd his lips on that unworthy place,
As it rain'd kisses.

Enter Antony and Domitius.

ANTONY: Favours, by Jove that thunders!
What art thou, fellow?

THIDIAS: One that but performs
The bidding of the fullest man, and worthiest
To have command obey'd.

DOMITIUS: You will be whipp'd.

ANTONY: Approach, there! Ah, you kite! Now, gods and devils!
Authority melts from me: of late, when I cried 'Ho!'
Like boys unto a muss, kings would start forth,
And cry 'Your will?' Have you no ears? I am Antony yet.

Enter Attendants.

Take hence this Jack, and whip him.

DOMITIUS: 'Tis better playing with a lion's whelp
Than with an old one dying.

ANTONY: Moon and stars!
Whip him. Were't twenty of the greatest tributaries
That do acknowledge Caesar, should I find them
So saucy with the hand of she here—what's her name,
Since she was Cleopatra? Whip him, fellows,
Till, like a boy, you see him cringe his face,
And whine aloud for mercy: take him hence.

THIDIAS: Mark Antony!

ANTONY: Tug him away: being whipp'd,
Bring him again: this Jack of Caesar's shall
Bear us an errand to him.
Exeunt Attendants with Thidias.
You were half blasted ere I knew you: ha!
Have I my pillow left unpress'd in Rome,
Forborne the getting of a lawful race,
And by a gem of women, to be abus'd
By one that looks on feeders?

CLEOPATRA: Good my Lord –
ANTONY: You have been a boggler ever:
 But when we in our viciousness grow hard –
 O misery on't! – the wise gods seel our eyes;
 In our own filth drop our clear judgments; make us
 Adore our errors; laugh at's, while we strut
 To our confusion.
CLEOPATRA: O, is't come to this?
ANTONY: I found you as a morsel, cold upon
 Dead Caesar's trencher; nay, you were a fragment
 Of Cneius Pompey's; besides what hotter hours,
 Unregister'd in vulgar fame, you have
 Luxuriously pick'd out: for, I am sure,
 Though you can guess what temperance should be,
 You know not what it is.
CLEOPATRA: Wherefore is this?
ANTONY: To let a fellow that will take rewards,
 And say 'God quit you!' be familiar with
 My playfellow, your hand; this kingly seal
 And plighter of high hearts! O, that I were
 Upon the hill of Basan, to outroar
 The horned herd! for I have savage cause;
 And to proclaim it civilly, were like
 A halter'd neck which does the hangman thank
 For being yare about him.
 Enter Attendants with Thidias.
 Is he whipp'd?
First Attendant: Soundly, my Lord.
ANTONY: Cried he? and begg'd a' pardon?
First Attendant: He did ask favour.
ANTONY: If that thy father live, let him repent
 Thou wast not made his daughter; and be thou sorry
 To follow Caesar in his triumph, since
 Thou hast been whipp'd for following him: henceforth

The white hand of a lady fever thee,
Shake thou to look on 't. Get thee back to Caesar,
Tell him thy entertainment: look, thou say
He makes me angry with him; for he seems
Proud and disdainful, harping on what I am,
Not what he knew I was: he makes me angry;
And at this time most easy 'tis to do't,
When my good stars, that were my former guides,
Have empty left their orbs, and shot their fires
Into the abysm of hell. If he mislike
My speech and what is done, tell him he has
Hipparchus, my enfranched bondman, whom
He may at pleasure whip, or hang, or torture,
As he shall like to quit me: urge it thou:
Hence with thy stripes, begone!

Exit Thidias.

CLEOPATRA: Have you done yet?
ANTONY: Alack, our terrene moon
Is now eclipsed; and it portends alone
The fall of Antony!
CLEOPATRA: I must stay his time.
ANTONY: To flatter Caesar, would you mingle eyes
With one that ties his points?
CLEOPATRA: Not know me yet?
ANTONY: Cold-hearted toward me?
CLEOPATRA: Ah, dear, if I be so,
From my cold heart let heaven engender hail,
And poison it in the source; and the first stone
Drop in my neck: as it determines, so
Dissolve my life! The next Caesarion smite!
Till by degrees the memory of my womb,
Together with my brave Egyptians all,
By the discandying of this pelleted storm,
Lie graveless, till the flies and gnats of Nile
Have buried them for prey!

ANTONY: I am satisfied.
Caesar sits down in Alexandria; where
I will oppose his fate. Our force by land
Hath nobly held; our sever'd navy too
Have knit again, and fleet, threatening most sea-like.
Where hast thou been, my heart? Dost thou hear, Lady?
If from the field I shall return once more
To kiss these lips, I will appear in blood;
I and my sword will earn our chronicle:
There's hope in't yet.
CLEOPATRA: That's my brave Lord!
ANTONY: I will be treble-sinew'd, heart'd, breath'd,
And fight maliciously: for when mine hours
Were nice and lucky, men did ransom lives
Of me for jests; but now I'll set my teeth,
And send to darkness all that stop me. Come,
Let's have one other gaudy night: call to me
All my sad captains; fill our bowls once more;
Let's mock the midnight bell.
CLEOPATRA: It is my birth-day:
I had thought to have held it poor: but, since my Lord
Is Antony again, I will be Cleopatra.
ANTONY: We will yet do well.
CLEOPATRA: Call all his noble captains to my Lord.
ANTONY: Do so, we'll speak to them; and to-night I'll force
The wine peep through their scars. Come on, my Queen;
There's sap in't yet. The next time I do fight,
I'll make death love me; for I will contend
Even with his pestilent scythe.
Exeunt all but Domitius.

DOMITIUS: Now he'll outstare the lightning. To be furious,
Is to be frighted out of fear; and in that mood
The dove will peck the estridge; and I see still,
A diminution in our captain's brain
Restores his heart: when valour preys on reason,
It eats the sword it fights with. I will seek
Some way to leave him.

Exit.

IV. 1

Enter Caesar, Agrippa and Maecenas, with his army; Caesar reading a letter.

CAESAR: He calls me boy; and chides, as he had power
To beat me out of Egypt; my messenger
He hath whipp'd with rods; dares me to personal combat,
Caesar to Antony: let the old ruffian know
I have many other ways to die; meantime
Laugh at his challenge.

MAECENAS: Caesar must think,
When one so great begins to rage, he's hunted
Even to falling. Give him no breath, but now
Make boot of his distraction: never anger
Made good guard for itself.

CAESAR: Let our best heads
Know, that to-morrow the last of many battles
We mean to fight: within our files there are,
Of those that served Mark Antony but late,
Enough to fetch him in. See it done:
And feast the army; we have store to do't,
And they have earn'd the waste. Poor Antony!

Exeunt.

IV. 2

Enter Antony, Cleopatra, Domitius, Charmian, Iras, Alexas, with others.

ANTONY: He will not fight with me, Domitius.
DOMITIUS: No.
ANTONY: Why should he not?
DOMITIUS: He thinks, being twenty times of better fortune,
He is twenty men to one.
ANTONY: To-morrow, soldier,
By sea and land I'll fight: or I will live,
Or bathe my dying honour in the blood
Shall make it live again. Woo't thou fight well?
DOMITIUS: I'll strike, and cry 'Take all.'
ANTONY: Well said; come on.
Call forth my household servants: let's to-night
Be bounteous at our meal.
Enter three or four Servitors.
Give me thy hand,
Thou hast been rightly honest—so hast thou—
Thou—and thou—and thou—you have serv'd me well,
And kings have been your fellows.
CLEOPATRA: What means this?
DOMITIUS: 'Tis one of those odd
tricks which sorrow shoots
Out of the mind.
ANTONY: And thou art honest too.
I wish I could be made so many men,
And all of you clapp'd up together, in
An Antony, that I might do you service
So good as you have done.
All: The gods forbid!
ANTONY: Well, my good fellows, wait on me to-night:
Scant not my cups; and make as much of me

As when mine Empire was your fellow too,
And suffer'd my command.
CLEOPATRA: What does he mean?
DOMITIUS: To make his followers weep.
ANTONY: Tend me to-night;
May be it is the period of your duty:
Haply you shall not see me more; or if,
A mangled shadow: perchance to-morrow
You'll serve another master. I look on you
As one that takes his leave. Mine honest friends,
I turn you not away; but, like a Master
Married to your good service, stay till death:
Tend me to-night two hours, I ask no more,
And the gods yield you for't!
DOMITIUS: What mean you, sir,
To give them this discomfort? Look, they weep;
And I, an ass, am onion-ey'd: for shame,
Transform us not to women.
ANTONY: Ho, ho, ho!
Now the witch take me, if I meant it thus!
Grace grow where those drops fall!
My hearty friends,
You take me in too dolorous a sense;
For I spake to you for your comfort; did desire you
To burn this night with torches: know, my hearts,
I hope well of to-morrow; and will lead you,
Where rather I'll expect victorious life
Than death and honour. Let's to supper, come,
And drown consideration.

Exeunt.

IV. 3

Enter a company of Soldiers.

First Soldier: Brother, good night: to-morrow is the day.

Second Soldier: It will determine one way: fare you well.
Heard you of nothing strange about the streets?
First Soldier: Nothing. What news?
Second Soldier: Belike 'tis but a rumour. Good night to you.
First Soldier: Well, sir, good night.

Enter two other Soldiers.

Second Soldier: Soldiers, have careful watch.
Third Soldier: And you. Good night, good night.
They place themselves in every corner of the stage.
Fourth Soldier: Here we: and if to-morrow
Our navy thrive, I have an absolute hope
Our landmen will stand up.
Third Soldier: 'Tis a brave army,
And full of purpose.
Music of the hautboys is under the stage.
Fourth Soldier: Peace! what noise?
First Soldier: List, list!
Second Soldier: Hark!
First Soldier: Music i' th' air.
Third Soldier: Under the earth.
Fourth Soldier: It signs well, does it not?
Third Soldier: No.
First Soldier: Peace, I say!
What should this mean?
Second Soldier: 'Tis the god Hercules, whom Antony loved,
Now leaves him.
First Soldier: Walk; let's see if other watchmen
Do hear what we do?
They advance to another post.
Second Soldier: How now, masters!
All: How now!
How now! do you hear this?

First Soldier: Ay; is't not strange?
Third Soldier: Do you hear, masters? do you hear?
First Soldier: Follow the noise so far as we have quarter;
Let's see how it will give off.
All: Content. 'Tis strange.

Exeunt.

IV. 4

Enter Antony and Cleopatra, Charmian and others attending.

ANTONY: Eros! mine armour, Eros!
CLEOPATRA: Sleep a little.
ANTONY: No, my chuck. Eros, come; mine armour, Eros!

Enter Eros with armour.

Come good fellow, put mine iron on:
If fortune be not ours to-day, it is
Because we brave her: come.
CLEOPATRA: Nay, I'll help too, Antony.
What's this for?
ANTONY: Ah, let be, let be! thou art
The armourer of my heart: false, false; this, this.
CLEOPATRA: Sooth, la, I'll help: thus it must be.
ANTONY: Well, well;
We shall thrive now. Seest thou, my good fellow?
Go put on thy defences.
EROS: Briefly, sir.
CLEOPATRA: Is not this buckled well?
ANTONY: Rarely, rarely:
He that unbuckles this, till we do please
To daff't for our repose, shall hear a storm.
Thou fumblest, Eros; and my Queen's a squire
More tight at this than thou: dispatch. O love,
That thou couldst see my wars to-day, and knew'st

The royal occupation! thou shouldst see
A workman in't.
Enter an armed Soldier.
Good morrow to thee; welcome:
Thou look'st like him that knows a warlike charge:
To business that we love we rise betime,
And go to't with delight.
Soldier: A thousand, sir,
Early though't be, have on their riveted trim,
And at the port expect you.
Shout. Trumpets flourish.
Enter Captains and Soldiers.
ALEXAS: The morn is fair. Good morrow, General.
All: Good morrow, General.
ANTONY: 'Tis well blown, lads:
This morning, like the spirit of a youth
That means to be of note, begins betimes.
So, so; come, give me that: this way; well said.
Fare thee well, dame, whate'er becomes of me:
This is a soldier's kiss: rebukeable,
And worthy shameful check it were, to stand
On more mechanic compliment; I'll leave thee
Now, like a man of steel. You that will fight,
Follow me close; I'll bring you to't. Adieu.
Exeunt All.
CHARMIAN: Please you, retire to your chamber.
CLEOPATRA: Lead me.
He goes forth gallantly. That he and Caesar might
Determine this great war in single fight!
Then Antony—but now—Well, on.
Exeunt.

IV. 5

Trumpets sound. Enter Antony, Eros and a Soldier.
Soldier: The gods make this a happy day to Antony!

ANTONY: Would thou and those thy scars had once prevail'd
To make me fight at land!
EROS: Hadst thou done so,
The kings that have revolted, and the soldier
That has this morning left thee, would have still
Follow'd thy heels.
ANTONY: Who's gone this morning?
Soldier: Who!
One ever near thee: call for Enobarbus,
He shall not hear thee; or from Caesar's camp,
Say 'I am none of thine.'
ANTONY: What say'st thou?
Soldier: Sir,
He is with Caesar.
EROS: Sir, his chests and treasure
He has not with him.
ANTONY: Is he gone?
Soldier: Most certain.
ANTONY: Go, Eros, send his treasure after; do it;
Detain no jot, I charge thee: write to him—
I will subscribe—gentle adieus and greetings;
Say that I wish he never find more cause
To change a Master. O, my fortunes have
Corrupted honest men! Dispatch.—Enobarbus!
Exeunt.

IV. 6

Flourish. Enter Caesar, Agrippa, with Domitius and others.

CAESAR: Go forth, Agrippa, and begin the fight:
Our will is Antony be took alive;
Make it so known.
AGRIPPA: Caesar, I shall.
Exit.

CAESAR: The time of universal peace is near:
Prove this a prosp'rous day, the three-nook'd world
Shall bear the olive freely.

Enter a Messenger.

Messenger: Antony
Is come into the field.
CAESAR: Go charge Agrippa
Plant those that have revolted in the vant,
That Antony may seem to spend his fury
Upon himself.

Exeunt all but Domitius.

DOMITIUS: Alexas did revolt; and went to Jewry on
Affairs of Antony; there did persuade
Great Herod to incline himself to Caesar,
And leave his Master Antony: for this pains
Caesar hath hang'd him. Canidius and the rest
That fell away, have entertainment, but
No honourable trust. I have done ill;
Of which I do accuse myself so sorely,
That I will joy no more.

Enter a Soldier of Caesar's.

Soldier: Enobarbus, Antony
Hath after thee sent all thy treasure, with
His bounty overplus: the messenger
Came on my guard; and at thy tent is now
Unloading of his mules.
DOMITIUS: I give it you.
Soldier: Mock not, Enobarbus.
I tell you true: best you saf'd the bringer
Out of the host; I must attend mine office,
Or would have done't myself. Your Emperor
Continues still a Jove.

Exit.

DOMITIUS: I am alone the villain of the earth,
And feel I am so most. O Antony,

Thou mine of bounty, how wouldst thou have paid
My better service, when my turpitude
Thou dost so crown with gold! This blows my heart:
If swift thought break it not, a swifter mean
Shall outstrike thought: but thought will do't, I feel.
I fight against thee! No: I will go seek
Some ditch wherein to die; the foul'st best fits
My latter part of life.

Exit.

IV. 7

Alarum. Drums and trumpets. Enter Agrippa.

AGRIPPA: Retire, we have engag'd ourselves too far:
Caesar himself has work, and our oppression
Exceeds what we expected.

Exeunt.

Alarums. Enter Antony and Scarus wounded.

SCARUS: O my brave Emperor, this is fought indeed!
Had we done so at first, we had droven them home
With clouts about their heads.

ANTONY: Thou bleed'st apace.

SCARUS: I had a wound here that was like a T,
But now 'tis made an H.

ANTONY: They do retire.

SCARUS: We'll beat 'em into bench-holes: I have yet
Room for six scotches more.

Enter Eros.

EROS: They are beaten, sir, and our advantage serves
For a fair victory.

SCARUS: Let us score their backs,
And snatch 'em up, as we take hares, behind:
'Tis sport to maul a runner.

ANTONY: I will reward thee

Once for thy spritely comfort, and ten-fold
For thy good valour. Come thee on.
SCARUS: I'll halt after.

Exeunt.

IV. 8

Alarum. Enter Antony, in a march; Scarus, with others.

ANTONY: We have beat him to his camp: run one before,
And let the Queen know of our guests. To-morrow,
Before the sun shall see 's, we'll spill the blood
That has to-day escap'd. I thank you all;
For doughty-handed are you, and have fought
Not as you serv'd the cause, but as 't had been
Each man's like mine; you have shown all Hectors.
Enter the city, clip your wives, your friends,
Tell them your feats; whilst they with joyful tears
Wash the congealment from your wounds, and kiss
The honour'd gashes whole.

Enter Cleopatra, attended.

Give me thy hand
To this great fairy I'll commend thy acts,
Make her thanks bless thee.
O thou day o' th' world,
Chain mine arm'd neck; leap thou, attire and all,
Through proof of harness to my heart, and there
Ride on the pants triumphing!
CLEOPATRA: Lord of lords!
O infinite virtue, com'st thou smiling from
The world's great snare uncaught.
ANTONY: My nightingale,
We have beat them to their beds.
What, girl! though grey
Do something mingle with our younger brown,
yet ha' we

A brain that nourishes our nerves, and can
Get goal for goal of youth. Behold this man;
Commend unto his lips thy favouring hand:
Kiss it, my warrior: he hath fought to-day
As if a god, in hate of mankind, had
Destroy'd in such a shape.
CLEOPATRA: I'll give thee, friend,
An armour all of gold; it was a king's.
ANTONY: He has deserv'd it, were it carbuncled
Like holy Phoebus' car. Give me thy hand:
Through Alexandria make a jolly march;
Bear our hack'd targets like the men that owe them:
Had our great Palace the capacity
To camp this host, we all would sup together,
And drink carouses to the next day's fate,
Which promises royal peril. Trumpeters,
With brazen din blast you the city's ear;
Make mingle with rattling tabourines;
That heaven and earth may strike their sounds together,
Applauding our approach.
Exeunt.

IV. 9

Sentinels at their post .

First ENTRY: If we be not relieved within this hour,
We must return to the court of guard: the night
Is shiny; and they say we shall embattle
By the second hour i' th' morn.
Second sENTRY: This last day was
A shrewd one to's.
Enter Domitius.
DOMITIUS: O, bear me witness, night–
Third sENTRY: What man is this?
Second sENTRY: Stand close, and list him.

DOMITIUS: Be witness to me, O thou blessed moon,
When men revolted shall upon record
Bear hateful memory, poor Enobarbus did
Before thy face repent!
First sENTRY: Enobarbus!
Third sENTRY: Peace!
Hark further.
DOMITIUS: O sovereign mistress of true melancholy,
The poisonous damp of night disponge upon me,
That life, a very rebel to my will,
May hang no longer on me: throw my heart
Against the flint and hardness of my fault:
Which, being dried with grief, will break to powder,
And finish all foul thoughts. O Antony,
Nobler than my revolt is infamous,
Forgive me in thine own particular;
But let the world rank me in register
A master-leaver and a fugitive:
O Antony! O Antony!
Second sENTRY: Let's speak to him.
First sENTRY: Let's hear him, for the things he speaks
May concern Caesar.
Third sENTRY: Let's do so. But he sleeps.
First sENTRY: Swoons rather; for so bad a prayer as his
Was never yet for sleep.
Second sENTRY: Go we to him.
Third sENTRY: Awake, sir, awake; speak to us.
Second sENTRY: Hear you, sir?
First sENTRY: The hand of death hath raught him.
Drums afar off.
Hark! the drums
Demurely wake the sleepers. Let us bear him
To the court of guard; he is of note: our hour
Is fully out.
Third sENTRY: Come on, then;

He may recover yet.

Exeunt with the body.

IV. 10

Enter Antony and Scarus, with their army.

ANTONY: Their preparation is to-day by sea;
We please them not by land.
SCARUS: For both, my Lord.
ANTONY: I would they'ld fight i' th' fire or i' th' air;
We'ld fight there too. But this it is; our foot
Upon the hills adjoining to the city
Shall stay with us: order for sea is given;
They have put forth the haven
Where their appointment we may best discover,
And look on their endeavour.

Exeunt.

IV. 11

Enter Caesar and his army.

CAESAR: But being charged, we will be still by land,
Which, as I take't, we shall; for his best force
Is forth to man his galleys. To the vales,
And hold our best advantage.

Exeunt.

IV. 12

Alarum far off, as at a sea-fight.
Enter Antony and Scarus.

ANTONY: Yet they are not join'd: where yond pine does stand,
I shall discover all: I'll bring thee word
Straight, how 'tis like to go.

Exit.

SCARUS: Swallows have built
In Cleopatra's sails their nests: the augurers
Say they know not, they cannot tell; look grimly,
And dare not speak their knowledge. Antony
Is valiant, and dejected; and, by starts,
His fretted fortunes give him hope, and fear,
Of what he has, and has not.

Enter Antony.

ANTONY: All is lost;
This foul Egyptian hath betrayed me:
My fleet hath yielded to the foe; and yonder
They cast their caps up and carouse together
Like friends long lost. Triple-turn'd whore! 'tis thou
Hast sold me to this novice; and my heart
Makes only wars on thee. Bid them all fly;
For when I am revenged upon my charm,
I have done all. Bid them all fly; begone.

Exit Scarus.

O sun, thy uprise shall I see no more:
Fortune and Antony part here; even here
Do we shake hands. All come to this? The hearts
That spaniel'd me at heels, to whom I gave
Their wishes, do discandy, melt their sweets
On blossoming Caesar; and this pine is bark'd,
That overtopp'd them all. Betray'd I am:
O this false soul of Egypt! this grave charm—
Whose eye beck'd forth my wars, and call'd them home;
Whose bosom was my crownet, my chief end—
Like a right gipsy, hath, at fast and loose,
Beguiled me to the very heart of loss.
What, Eros, Eros!
Enter Cleopatra.
Ah, thou spell! Avaunt!

CLEOPATRA: Why is my Lord enrag'd against his love?

ANTONY: Vanish, or I shall give thee thy deserving,
And blemish Caesar's triumph. Let him take thee,
And hoist thee up to the shouting plebeians:
Follow his chariot, like the greatest spot
Of all thy sex; most monster-like, be shown
For poor'st diminutives, for dolts; and let
Patient Octavia plough thy visage up
With her prepared nails.

Exit Cleopatra.

'Tis well thou'rt gone,
If it be well to live; but better 'twere
Thou fell'st into my fury, for one death
Might have prevented many. Eros, ho!
The shirt of Nessus is upon me: teach me,
Alcides, thou mine ancestor, thy rage:
Let me lodge Lichas on the horns o' th' moon;
And with those hands, that grasp'd the heaviest club,
Subdue my worthiest self. The witch shall die:
To the young Roman boy she hath sold me, and I fall
Under this plot; she dies for't. Eros, ho!

Exit.

IV. 13

Enter Cleopatra, Charmian, Iras and Mardian.

CLEOPATRA: Help me, my women! O, he is more mad
Than Telamon for his shield; the boar of Thessaly
Was never so emboss'd.

CHARMIAN: To the monument!
There lock yourself, and send him word you are dead.

The soul and body rive not more in parting
Than greatness going off.
CLEOPATRA: To the monument!
Mardian, go tell him I have slain myself;
Say, that the last I spoke was 'Antony,'
And word it, prithee, piteously: hence, Mardian,
And bring me how he takes my death.
To the monument!
Exeunt.

IV. 14

Enter Antony and Eros.

ANTONY: Eros, thou yet behold'st me?
EROS: Ay, noble Lord.
ANTONY: Sometimes we see a cloud that's dragonish;
A vapour sometime like a bear or lion,
A tower'd citadel, a pendent rock,
A forked mountain, or blue promontory
With trees upon't, that nod unto the world,
And mock our eyes with air: thou hast seen these signs;
They are black vesper's pageants.
EROS: Ay, my Lord,
ANTONY: That which is now a horse, even with a thought
The rack dislimns, and makes it indistinct,
As water is in water.
EROS: It does, my Lord.
ANTONY: My good knave Eros, now thy captain is
Even such a body: here I am Antony:
Yet cannot hold this visible shape, my knave.
I made these wars for Egypt: and the Queen—
Whose heart I thought I had, for she had mine;
Which whilst it was mine had annex'd unto't
A million more, now lost—she, Eros, has

Pack'd cards with Caesar, and false-play'd my glory
Unto an enemy's triumph.
Nay, weep not, gentle Eros; there is left us
Ourselves to end ourselves.
Enter Mardian.
O! thy vile Lady!
She has robb'd me of my sword.

MARDIAN: No, Antony;
My mistress loved thee, and her fortunes mingled
With thine entirely.

ANTONY: Hence, saucy eunuch; peace!
She hath betray'd me and shall die the death.

MARDIAN: Death of one person can be paid but once,
And that she has discharg'd: what thou wouldst do
Is done unto thy hand: the last she spake
Was 'Antony! most noble Antony!'
Then in the midst a tearing groan did break
The name of Antony; it was divided
Between her heart and lips: she render'd life,
Thy name so buried in her.

ANTONY: Dead, then?

MARDIAN: Dead.

ANTONY: Unarm, Eros; the long day's task is done,
And we must sleep.
That thou depart'st hence safe,
Does pay thy labour richly; go.

Exit Mardian.

The seven-fold shield of Ajax cannot keep
The battery from my heart. O, cleave, my sides!
Heart, once be stronger than thy continent,
Crack thy frail case! Apace, Eros, apace.
No more a soldier: bruised pieces, go;
You have been nobly borne. From me awhile.
Exit Eros.
I will o'ertake thee, Cleopatra, and

Weep for my pardon. So it must be, for now
All length is torture: since the torch is out,
Lie down, and stray no farther: now all labour
Mars what it does; yea, very force entangles
Itself with strength: seal then, and all is done.
Eros!—I come, my queen:—Eros!—Stay for me:
Where souls do couch on flowers, we'll hand in hand,
And with our sprightly port make the ghosts gaze:
Dido and her AEneas shall want troops,
And all the haunt be ours. Come, Eros, Eros!

Enter Eros.

EROS: What would my Lord?

ANTONY: Since Cleopatra died,
I have liv'd in such dishonour, that the gods
Detest my baseness. I, that with my sword
Quarter'd the world, and o'er green Neptune's back
With ships, made cities, condemn myself, to lack
The courage of a woman; less noble mind
Than she which by her death our Caesar tells
'I am conqueror of myself.' Thou art sworn, Eros,
That, when the exigent should come, which now
Is come indeed, when I should see behind me
The inevitable prosecution of
Disgrace and horror, that, on my command,
Thou then wouldst kill me: do't; the time is come:
Thou strikest not me, 'tis Caesar thou defeat'st.
Put colour in thy cheek.

EROS: The gods withhold me!
Shall I do that which all the Parthian darts,
Though enemy, lost aim, and could not?

ANTONY: Eros,
Wouldst thou be window'd in great Rome and see
Thy master thus with pleach'd arms, bending down
His corrigible neck, his face subdu'd

To penetrative shame, whilst the wheel'd seat
Of fortunate Caesar, drawn before him, branded
His baseness that ensued?
EROS: I would not see't.
ANTONY: Come, then; for with a wound I must be cur'd.
Draw that thy honest sword, which thou hast worn
Most useful for thy country.
EROS: O, sir, pardon me!
ANTONY: When I did make thee free, sworest thou not then
To do this when I bade thee? Do it at once;
Or thy precedent services are all
But accidents unpurpos'd. Draw, and come.
EROS: Turn from me, then, that noble countenance,
Wherein the worship of the whole world lies.
ANTONY: Lo thee!
Turning from him
EROS: My sword is drawn.
ANTONY: Then let it do at once
The thing why thou hast drawn it.
EROS: My dear Master,
My Captain, and my Emperor, let me say,
Before I strike this bloody stroke, farewell.
ANTONY: 'Tis said, man; and farewell.
EROS: Farewell, great chief. Shall I strike now?
ANTONY: Now, Eros.
EROS: Why, there then: thus I do escape the sorrow
Of Antony's death.
Kills himself.
ANTONY: Thrice-nobler than myself!
Thou teachest me, O valiant Eros, what
I should, and thou couldst not. My Queen and Eros
Have by their brave instruction got upon me
A nobleness in record: but I will be

A bridegroom in my death, and run into't
As to a lover's bed. Come, then; and, Eros,
Thy Master dies thy scholar: to do thus
Falling on his sword.
I learn'd of thee. How! not dead? not dead?
The guard, ho! O, dispatch me!

Enter Dercetas and Guard.

First Guard: What's the noise?

ANTONY: I have done my work in, friends: O, make an end
Of what I have begun.

Second Guard: The star is fall'n.

First Guard: And time is at his period.

All: Alas, and woe!

ANTONY: Let him that loves me strike me dead.

First Guard: Not I.

Second Guard: Nor I.

Third Guard: Nor any one.

Exeunt Guard.

DERCETAS: Thy death and fortunes bid thy followers fly.
This sword but shown to Caesar, with this tidings,
Shall enter me with him.

Enter Diomedes.

DIOMEDES: Where's Antony?

DERCETAS: There, Diomed there.

DIOMEDES: Lives he?
Wilt thou not answer, man?

Exit Dercetas.

ANTONY: Art thou there, Diomed? Draw thy sword, and give me
Sufficing strokes for death.

DIOMEDES: Most absolute Lord,
My mistress Cleopatra sent me to thee.

ANTONY: When did she send thee?

DIOMEDES: Now, my Lord.
ANTONY: Where is she?
DIOMEDES: Lock'd in her monument. She had a prophesying fear
Of what hath come to pass: for when she saw—
Which never shall be found—you did suspect
She had dispos'd with Caesar, and that your rage
Would not be purg'd, she sent you word she was dead;
But, fearing since how it might work, hath sent
Me to proclaim the truth; and I am come,
I dread, too late.
ANTONY: Too late, good Diomed: call my guard, I prithee.
DIOMEDES: What, ho, the Emperor's guard! The guard, what, ho!
Come, your Lord calls!
Enter four or five of the Guard of Antony.
ANTONY: Bear me, good friends, where Cleopatra bides;
'Tis the last service that I shall command you.
First Guard: Woe, woe are we, sir, you may not live to wear
All your true followers out.
All: Most heavy day!
ANTONY: Nay, good my fellows, do not please sharp fate
To grace it with your sorrows: bid that welcome
Which comes to punish us, and we punish it
Seeming to bear it lightly. Take me up:
I have led you oft: carry me now, good friends,
And have my thanks for all.

Exeunt bearing Antony.

IV. 15

Enter Cleopatra and her maids aloft, with Charmian and Iras.

CLEOPATRA: O Charmian, I will never go from hence.
CHARMIAN: Be comforted, dear Madam.
CLEOPATRA: No, I will not:
All strange and terrible events are welcome,
But comforts we despise; our size of sorrow,
Proportion'd to our cause, must be as great
As that which makes it.

Enter Diomedes.

How now! is he dead?
DIOMEDES: His death's upon him, but not dead.
Look out o' th' other side your monument;
His guard have brought him thither.
Enter Antony and the Guard.
CLEOPATRA: O sun,
Burn the great sphere thou movest in! darkling stand
The varying shore o' th' world. O Antony,
Antony, Antony! Help, Charmian, help, Iras, help;
Help, friends below; let's draw him hither.
ANTONY: Peace!
Not Caesar's valour hath o'erthrown Antony,
But Antony's hath triumph'd on itself.
CLEOPATRA: So it should be, that none but Antony
Should conquer Antony; but woe 'tis so!
ANTONY: I am dying, Egypt, dying; only
I here importune death awhile, until
Of many thousand kisses the poor last
I lay up thy lips.
CLEOPATRA: I dare not, dear—
Dear my Lord, pardon—I dare not,
Lest I be taken: not the imperious show
Of the full-fortuned Caesar ever shall

Be brooch'd with me; if knife, drugs, serpents, have
Edge, sting, or operation, I am safe:
Your wife Octavia, with her modest eyes
And still conclusion, shall acquire no honour
Demuring upon me. But come, come, Antony –
Help me, my women – we must draw thee up:
Assist, good friends.
ANTONY: O, quick, or I am gone.
CLEOPATRA: Here's sport indeed!
How heavy weighs my Lord!
Our strength is all gone into heaviness,
That makes the weight: had I great Juno's power,
The strong-wing'd Mercury should fetch thee up,
And set thee by Jove's side. Yet come a little –
Wishes were ever fools – O, come, come, come;
They heave Antony aloft to Cleopatra.
And welcome, welcome! die where thou hast liv'd:
Quicken with kissing: had my lips that power,
Thus would I wear them out.
All: A heavy sight!
ANTONY: I am dying, Egypt, dying:
Give me some wine, and let me speak a little.
CLEOPATRA: No, let me speak; and let me rail so high,
That the false housewife Fortune break her wheel,
Provok'd by my offence.
ANTONY: One word, sweet Queen:
Of Caesar seek your honour, with your safety. O!
CLEOPATRA: They do not go together.
ANTONY: Gentle, hear me:
None about Caesar trust but Proculeius.
CLEOPATRA: My resolution and my hands I'll trust;
None about Caesar.
ANTONY: The miserable change now at my end
Lament nor sorrow at; but please your thoughts
In feeding them with those my former fortunes

Wherein I lived, the greatest prince o' th' world,
The noblest; and do now not basely die,
Not cowardly put off my helmet to
My countryman—a Roman by a Roman
Valiantly vanquish'd. Now my spirit is going;
I can do no more.

CLEOPATRA: Noblest of men, woo't die?
Hast thou no care of me? shall I abide
In this dull world, which in thy absence is
No better than a sty? O, see, my women,
Antony dies.
The crown o' th' earth doth melt. My Lord!
O, wither'd is the garland of the war,
The soldier's pole is fall'n: young boys and girls
Are level now with men; the odds is gone,
And there is nothing left remarkable
Beneath the visiting moon.

CHARMIAN: O, quietness, Lady!

IRAS: She is dead too, our sovereign.

CHARMIAN: Lady!

IRAS: Madam!

CHARMIAN: O Madam, Madam, Madam!

IRAS: Royal Egypt, Empress!

CHARMIAN: Peace, peace, Iras!

CLEOPATRA: No more, but e'en a woman, and commanded
By such poor passion as the maid that milks
And does the meanest chares. It were for me
To throw my sceptre at the injurious gods;
To tell them that this world did equal theirs
Till they had stol'n our jewel. All's but naught;
Patience is scottish, and impatience does
Become a dog that's mad: then is it sin
To rush into the secret house of death,
Ere death dare come to us? How do you, women?

What, what! good cheer! Why, how now, Charmian!
My noble girls! Ah, women, women, look,
Our lamp is spent, it's out! Good sirs, take heart:
We'll bury him; and then, what's brave, what's noble,
Let's do it after the high Roman fashion,
And make death proud to take us. Come, away:
This case of that huge spirit now is cold:
Ah, women, women! come; we have no friend
But resolution, and the briefest end.
Exeunt; bearing off Antony's body.

V. 1

Enter Caesar, Agrippa, Dolabella, Maecenas, Gallus, Proculeius and others, his council of war.

CAESAR: Go to him, Dolabella, bid him yield;
Being so frustrate, tell him he mocks
The pauses that he makes.
DOLABELLA: Caesar, I shall.

Exit.

Enter Dercetas, with the sword of Antony.

CAESAR: Wherefore is that? and what art thou that darest
Appear thus to us?
DERCETAS: I am call'd Dercetas;
Mark Antony I serv'd, who best was worthy
Best to be served: whilst he stood up and spoke,
He was my Master; and I wore my life
To spend upon his haters. If thou please
To take me to thee, as I was to him
I'll be to Caesar; if thou pleasest not,
I yield thee up my life.
CAESAR: What is't thou say'st?
DERCETAS: I say, O Caesar, Antony is dead.
CAESAR: The breaking of so great a thing should make

A greater crack: the round world
Should have shook lions into civil streets,
And citizens to their dens: the death of Antony
Is not a single doom; in the name lay
A moiety of the world.
DERCETAS: He is dead, Caesar:
Not by a public minister of justice,
Nor by a hired knife; but that self hand,
Which writ his honour in the acts it did,
Hath, with the courage which the heart did lend it,
Splitted the heart. This is his sword;
I robb'd his wound of it; behold it stain'd
With his most noble blood.
CAESAR: Look you sad, friends?
The gods rebuke me, but it is tidings
To wash the eyes of kings.
AGRIPPA: And strange it is,
That nature must compel us to lament
Our most persisted deeds.
MAECENAS: His taints and honours
Waged equal with him.
AGRIPPA: A rarer spirit never
Did steer humanity: but you, gods, will give us
Some faults to make us men. Caesar is touch'd.
MAECENAS: When such a spacious mirror's set before him,
He needs must see himself.
CAESAR: O Antony!
I have follow'd thee to this; but we do lance
Diseases in our bodies: I must perforce
Have shown to thee such a declining day,
Or look on thine; we could not stall together
In the whole world: but yet let me lament,
With tears as sovereign as the blood of hearts,
That thou, my brother, my competitor

In top of all design, my mate in Empire,
Friend and companion in the front of war,
The arm of mine own body, and the heart
Where mine his thoughts did kindle – that our stars,
Unreconcilable, should divide
Our equalness to this. Hear me, good friends –
But I will tell you at some meeter season,
Enter an Egyptian.
The business of this man looks out of him;
We'll hear him what he says. Whence are you?
Egyptian: A poor Egyptian yet. The Queen my mistress,
Confin'd in all she has, her monument,
Of thy intents desires instruction,
That she preparedly may frame herself
To the way she's forced to.
CAESAR: Bid her have good heart:
She soon shall know of us, by some of ours,
How honourable and how kindly we
Determine for her; for Caesar cannot live
To be ungentle.
Egyptian: So the gods preserve thee!
Exit.
CAESAR: Come hither, Proculeius. Go and say,
We purpose her no shame: give her what comforts
The quality of her passion shall require,
Lest, in her greatness, by some mortal stroke
She do defeat us; for her life in Rome
Would be eternal in our triumph: go,
And with your speediest bring us what she says,
And how you find of her.
PROCULEIUS: Caesar, I shall.
Exit.
CAESAR: Gallus, go you along.
Exit Gallus.

Where's Dolabella,
To second Proculeius?
All: Dolabella!
CAESAR: Let him alone, for I remember now
How he's employ'd: he shall in time be ready.
Go with me to my tent; where you shall see
How hardly I was drawn into this war;
How calm and gentle I proceeded still
In all my writings: go with me, and see
What I can show in this.
Exeunt.

V. 2

Enter Cleopatra, Charmian and Iras.
CLEOPATRA: My desolation does begin to make
A better life. 'Tis paltry to be Caesar;
Not being Fortune, he's but Fortune's knave,
A minister of her will: and it is great
To do that thing that ends all other deeds;
Which shackles accidents and bolts up change;
Which sleeps, and never palates more the dung,
The beggar's nurse and Caesar's.
Enter Proculeius, Gallus and Soldiers.
PROCULEIUS: Caesar sends greeting to the Queen of Egypt;
And bids thee study on what fair demands
Thou mean'st to have him grant thee.
CLEOPATRA: What's thy name?
PROCULEIUS: My name is Proculeius.
CLEOPATRA: Antony
Did tell me of you, bade me trust you; but
I do not greatly care to be deceiv'd,
That have no use for trusting. If your Master
Would have a Queen his beggar, you must tell him,
That majesty, to keep decorum, must

No less beg than a kingdom: if he please
To give me conquer'd Egypt for my son,
He gives me so much of mine own, as I
Will kneel to him with thanks.
PROCULEIUS: Be of good cheer;
You're fall'n into a princely hand, fear nothing:
Make your full reference freely to my Lord,
Who is so full of grace, that it flows over
On all that need: let me report to him
Your sweet dependency; and you shall find
A conqueror that will pray in aid for kindness,
Where he for grace is kneel'd to.
CLEOPATRA: Pray you, tell him
I am his fortune's vassal, and I send him
The greatness he has got. I hourly learn
A doctrine of obedience; and would gladly
Look him i' th' face.
PROCULEIUS: This I'll report, dear Lady.
Have comfort, for I know your plight is pitied
Of him that caus'd it.

Enter Soldies.

GALLUS: You see how easily she may be surprised:
Guard her till Caesar come.
IRAS: Royal Queen!
CHARMIAN: O Cleopatra! thou art taken, Queen:
CLEOPATRA: Quick, quick, good hands.
Drawing a dagger.
PROCULEIUS: Hold, worthy lady, hold:
Seizes and disarms her.
Do not yourself such wrong, who are in this
Reliev'd, but not betray'd.
CLEOPATRA: What, of death too,
That rids our dogs of languish?
PROCULEIUS: Cleopatra,
Do not abuse my Master's bounty, by

The undoing of yourself: let the world see
His nobleness well acted, which your death
Will never let come forth.

CLEOPATRA: Where art thou, death?
Come hither, come! come, come, and take a Queen
Worthy many babes and beggars!

PROCULEIUS: O, temperance, Lady!

CLEOPATRA: Sir, I will eat no meat, I'll not drink, sir;
If idle talk will once be necessary,
I'll not sleep neither: this mortal house I'll ruin,
Do Caesar what he can. Know, sir, that I
Will not wait pinion'd at your Master's court;
Nor once be chastised with the sober eye
Of dull Octavia. Shall they hoist me up
And show me to the shouting varletry
Of censuring Rome? Rather a ditch in Egypt
Be gentle grave unto me! rather on Nilus' mud
Lay me stark naked, and let the water-flies
Blow me into abhorring! rather make
My country's high pyramides my gibbet,
And hang me up in chains!

PROCULEIUS: You do extend
These thoughts of horror further than you shall
Find cause in Caesar.

Enter Dolabella.

DOLABELLA: Proculeius,
What thou hast done, thy Master Caesar knows,
And he hath sent for thee: for the Queen,
I'll take her to my guard.

PROCULEIUS: So, Dolabella,
It shall content me best: be gentle to her.
To Caesar I will speak what you shall please,
If you'll employ me to him.

CLEOPATRA: Say, I would die.

Exeunt Proculeius.

DOLABELLA: Most noble Empress, you have heard of me?
CLEOPATRA: I cannot tell.
DOLABELLA: Assuredly you know me.
CLEOPATRA: No matter, sir, what I have heard or known.
You laugh when boys or women tell their dreams;
Is't not your trick?
DOLABELLA: I understand not, Madam.
CLEOPATRA: I dream'd there was an Emperor Antony:
O, such another sleep, that I might see
But such another man!
DOLABELLA: If it might please ye—
CLEOPATRA: His face was as the heavens; and therein stuck
A sun and moon, which kept their course, and lighted
The little o' the earth.
DOLABELLA: Most sovereign creature—
CLEOPATRA: His legs bestrid the ocean: his rear'd arm
Crested the world: his voice was propertied
As all the tuned spheres, and that to friends;
But when he meant to quail and shake the Orb,
He was as rattling thunder. For his bounty,
There was no winter in't; an autumn 'twas,
That grew the more by reaping: his delights
Were dolphin-like; they show'd his back above
The element they lived in: in his livery
Walk'd crowns and crownets; realms and islands were
As plates dropp'd from his pocket.
DOLABELLA: Cleopatra!
CLEOPATRA: Think you there was, or might be, such

a man
As this I dream'd of?
DOLABELLA: Gentle Madam, no.
CLEOPATRA: You lie, up to the hearing of the gods.
But, if there be, or ever were, one such,
It's past the size of dreaming: nature wants stuff
To vie strange forms with fancy; yet, to imagine
And Antony, were nature's piece 'gainst fancy,
Condemning shadows quite.
DOLABELLA: Hear me, good Madam.
Your loss is as yourself, great; and you bear it
As answering to the weight: would I might never
O'ertake pursued success, but I do feel,
By the rebound of yours, a grief that smites
My very heart at root.
CLEOPATRA: I thank you, sir,
Know you what Caesar means to do with me?
DOLABELLA: I am loath to tell you what I would you knew.
CLEOPATRA: Nay, pray you, sir –
DOLABELLA: Though he be honourable –
CLEOPATRA: He'll lead me, then, in triumph?
DOLABELLA: Madam, he will; I know't.
Flourish, and shout within, 'Make way there: Octavius Caesar!'
Enter Caesar, Gallus, Proculeius, Maecenas, Seleucus, and others of his train.
CAESAR: Which is the Queen of Egypt?
DOLABELLA: It is the Emperor, Madam.
Cleopatra kneels.
CAESAR: Arise, you shall not kneel:
I pray you, rise; rise, Egypt.
CLEOPATRA: Sir, the gods
Will have it thus; my Master and my Lord
I must obey.

CAESAR: Take to you no hard thoughts:
The record of what injuries you did us,
Though written in our flesh, we shall remember
As things but done by chance.
CLEOPATRA: Sole sir o' th' world,
I cannot project mine own cause so well
To make it clear; but do confess I have
Been laden with like frailties which before
Have often shamed our sex.
CAESAR: Cleopatra, know,
We will extenuate rather than enforce:
If you apply yourself to our intents,
Which towards you are most gentle, you shall find
A benefit in this change; but if you seek
To lay on me a cruelty, by taking
Antony's course, you shall bereave yourself
Of my good purposes, and put your children
To that destruction which I'll guard them from,
If thereon you rely. I'll take my leave.
CLEOPATRA: And may, through all the world: 'tis yours; and we, Your scutcheons and your signs of conquest, shall Hang in what place you please. Here, my good Lord.
CAESAR: You shall advise me in all for Cleopatra.
CLEOPATRA: This is the brief of money, plate, and jewels, I am possess'd of: 'tis exactly valued;
Not petty things admitted. Where's Seleucus?
SELEUCUS: Here, Madam.
CLEOPATRA: This is my treasurer: let him speak, my Lord, Upon his peril, that I have reserv'd
To myself nothing. Speak the truth, Seleucus.
SELEUCUS: Madam,
I had rather seal my lips, than, to my peril,
Speak that which is not.
CLEOPATRA: What have I kept back?

SELEUCUS: Enough to purchase what you have made
known.

CAESAR: Nay, blush not, Cleopatra; I approve
Your wisdom in the deed.

CLEOPATRA: See, Caesar! O, behold,
How pomp is follow'd! mine will now be yours;
And, should we shift estates, yours would be mine.
The ingratitude of this Seleucus does
Even make me wild: O slave, of no more trust
Than love that's hired! What, goest thou back? thou
shalt
Go back, I warrant thee; but I'll catch thine eyes,
Though they had wings: slave, soulless villain, dog!
O rarely base!

CAESAR: Good Queen, let us entreat you.

CLEOPATRA: O Caesar, what a wounding shame is
this, That thou, vouchsafing here to visit me,
Doing the honour of thy lordliness
To one so meek, that mine own servant should
Parcel the sum of my disgraces by
Addition of his envy! Say, good Caesar,
That I some lady trifles have reserv'd,
Immoment toys, things of such dignity
As we greet modern friends withal; and say,
Some nobler token I have kept apart
For Livia and Octavia, to induce
Their mediation; must I be unfolded
With one that I have bred? The gods! it smites me
Beneath the fall I have.
Prithee, go hence;
Or I shall show the cinders of my spirits
Through the ashes of my chance: wert thou a man,
Thou wouldst have mercy on me.

CAESAR: Forbear, Seleucus.

Exit Seleucus.

CLEOPATRA: Be it known, that we, the greatest, are misthought
For things that others do; and, when we fall,
We answer others' merits in our name,
Are therefore to be pitied.
CAESAR: Cleopatra,
Not what you have reserv'd, nor what acknowledg'd,
Put we i' th' roll of conquest: still be't yours,
Bestow it at your pleasure; and believe,
Caesar's no merchant, to make prize with you
Of things that merchants sold. Therefore be cheer'd;
Make not your thoughts your prisons: no, dear Queen;
For we intend so to dispose you as
Yourself shall give us counsel. Feed, and sleep:
Our care and pity is so much upon you,
That we remain your friend; and so, adieu.
CLEOPATRA: My Master, and my Lord!
CAESAR: Not so. Adieu.

Flourish. Exeunt Caesar and his train.

CLEOPATRA: He words me, girls, he words me, that I should not
Be noble to myself: but, hark thee, Charmian.
IRAS: Finish, good Lady; the bright day is done,
And we are for the dark.
CLEOPATRA: Hie thee again:
I have spoke already, and it is provided;
Go put it to the haste.
CHARMIAN: Madam, I will.

Enter Dolabella.

DOLABELLA: Where is the Queen?
CHARMIAN: Behold, sir.

Exit.

CLEOPATRA: Dolabella!
DOLABELLA: Madam, as thereto sworn by your

command, Which my love makes religion to obey,
I tell you this: Caesar through Syria
Intends his journey; and within three days
You with your children will he send before:
Make your best use of this: I have perform'd
Your pleasure and my promise.
CLEOPATRA: Dolabella,
I shall remain your debtor.
DOLABELLA: I your servant,
Adieu, good Queen; I must attend on Caesar.
CLEOPATRA: Farewell, and thanks.
Exit Dolabella.
Now, Iras, what think'st thou?
Thou, an Egyptian puppet, shalt be shown
In Rome, as well as I, mechanic slaves
With greasy aprons, rules, and hammers, shall
Uplift us to the view; in their thick breaths,
Rank of gross diet, shall be enclouded,
And forc'd to drink their vapour.
IRAS: The gods forbid!
CLEOPATRA: Nay, 'tis most certain, Iras: saucy lictors
Will catch at us, like strumpets; and scald rhymers
Ballad us out o' tune: the quick comedians
Extemporally will stage us, and present
Our Alexandrian revels; Antony
Shall be brought drunken forth, and I shall see
Some squeaking Cleopatra boy my greatness
I' th' posture of a whore.
IRAS: O the good gods!
CLEOPATRA: Nay, that's certain.
IRAS: I'll never see 't; for, I am sure, my nails
Are stronger than mine eyes.
CLEOPATRA: Why, that's the way
To fool their preparation, and to conquer
Their most absurd intents.

Enter Charmian.
Now, Charmian!
Show me, my women, like a queen: go fetch
My best attires: I am again for Cydnus,
To meet Mark Antony: sirrah Iras, go.
Now, noble Charmian, we'll dispatch indeed;
And, when thou hast done this chare, I'll give thee leave
To play till Doomsday. Bring our crown and all.
Exit Iras. A noise within.
Wherefore's this noise?
Enter a Guardsman.
Guard: Here is a rural fellow
That will not be denied your Highness presence:
He brings you figs.
CLEOPATRA: Let him come in.
Exit Guardsman.
What poor an instrument
May do a noble deed! he brings me liberty.
My resolution's placed, and I have nothing
Of woman in me: now from head to foot
I am marble-constant; now the fleeting moon
No planet is of mine.
Enter Guardsman with Clown bringing in a basket.
Guard: This is the man.
CLEOPATRA: Avoid, and leave him.
Exit Guardsman.
Hast thou the pretty worm of Nilus there,
That kills and pains not?
Clown: Truly, I have him: but I would not be the party that should desire you to touch him, for his biting is immortal; those that do die of it, do seldom or never recover.
CLEOPATRA: Rememberest thou any that have died on't?

Clown: Very many, men and women too. I heard of one of them no longer than yesterday: a very honest woman, but something given to lie; as a woman should not do, but in the way of honesty: how she died of the biting of it, what pain she felt: truly, she makes a very good report o' th' worm; but he that will believe all that they say, shall never be saved by half that they do: but this is most fallible, the worm's an odd worm.

CLEOPATRA: Get thee hence; farewell.

Clown: I wish you all joy of the worm.

CLEOPATRA: Farewell.

Clown: You must think this, look you, that the worm will do his kind.

CLEOPATRA: Ay, ay; farewell.

Clown: Look you, the worm is not to be trusted but in the keeping of wise people; for, indeed, there is no goodness in worm.

CLEOPATRA: Take thou no care; it shall be heeded.

Clown: Very good. Give it nothing, I pray you, for it is not worth the feeding.

CLEOPATRA: Will it eat me?

Clown: You must not think I am so simple but I know the devil himself will not eat a woman: I know that a woman is a dish for the gods, if the devil dress her not. But, truly, these same whoreson devils do the gods great harm in their women; for in every ten that they make, the devils mar five.

CLEOPATRA: Well, get thee gone; farewell.

Clown: Yes, forsooth: I wish you joy o' th' worm.

Exit.

Enter Iras.

CLEOPATRA: Give me my robe, put on my crown; I have Immortal longings in me: now no more
The juice of Egypt's grape shall moist this lip:

Yare, yare, good Iras; quick. Methinks I hear
Antony call; I see him rouse himself
To praise my noble act; I hear him mock
The luck of Caesar, which the gods give men
To excuse their after wrath: husband, I come:
Now to that name my courage prove my title!
I am fire and air; my other elements
I give to baser life. So; have you done?
Come then, and take the last warmth of my lips.
Farewell, kind Charmian; Iras, long farewell.
Kisses them. Iras falls and dies.
Have I the aspic in my lips? Dost fall?
If thou and nature can so gently part,
The stroke of death is as a lover's pinch,
Which hurts, and is desired. Dost thou lie still?
If thus thou vanishest, thou tell'st the world
It is not worth leave-taking.

CHARMIAN: Dissolve, thick cloud, and rain; that I may say, The gods themselves do weep!

CLEOPATRA: This proves me base:
If she first meet the curled Antony,
He'll make demand of her, and spend that kiss
Which is my heaven to have. Come, thou mortal wretch,
To an asp, which she applies to her breast.
With thy sharp teeth this knot intrinsicate
Of life at once untie: poor venomous fool
Be angry, and dispatch. O, couldst thou speak,
That I might hear thee call great Caesar ass
Unpolicied!

CHARMIAN: O Eastern Star!

CLEOPATRA: Peace, peace!
Dost thou not see my baby at my breast,
That sucks the nurse asleep?

CHARMIAN: O, break! O, break!

CLEOPATRA: As sweet as balm, as soft as air, as gentle,—
O Antony!—Nay, I will take thee too.
What should I stay—
Dies.
CHARMIAN: In this vile world? So, fare thee well.
Now boast thee, death, in thy possession lies
A lass unparallel'd. Downy windows, close;
And golden Phoebus never be beheld
Of eyes again so royal! Your crown's awry;
I'll mend it, and then play.

Enter the Guards, rushing in.

First Guard: Where is the Queen?
CHARMIAN: Speak softly, wake her not.
First Guard: Caesar hath sent—
CHARMIAN: Too slow a messenger.
Applies an asp.
O, come apace, dispatch! I partly feel thee.
First Guard: Approach, ho! All's not well: Caesar's beguiled.
Second Guard: There's Dolabella sent from Caesar; call him.
First Guard: What work is here! Charmian, is this well done?
CHARMIAN: It is well done, and fitting for a princess
Descended of so many royal kings.
Ah, soldier!
Charmian dies.

Enter Dolabella.

DOLABELLA: How goes it here?
Second Guard: All dead.
DOLABELLA: Caesar, thy thoughts
Touch their effects in this: thyself art coming
To see perform'd the dreaded act which thou
So sought'st to hinder.

Enter Caesar and all his train marching.

DOLABELLA: O sir, you are too sure an augurer;
That you did fear is done.
CAESAR: Bravest at the last,
She levell'd at our purposes, and, being royal,
Took her own way. The manner of their deaths?
I do not see them bleed.
DOLABELLA: Who was last with them?
First Guard: A simple countryman, that brought her figs:
This was his basket.
CAESAR: Poison'd, then.
First Guard: O Caesar,
This Charmian liv'd but now; she stood and spake:
I found her trimming up the diadem
On her dead mistress; tremblingly she stood
And on the sudden dropp'd.
CAESAR: O noble weakness!
If they had swallow'd poison, 'twould appear
By external swelling: but she looks like sleep,
As she would catch another Antony
In her strong toil of grace.
DOLABELLA: Here, on her breast,
There is a vent of blood and something blown:
The like is on her arm.
First Guard: This is an aspic's trail: and these fig-leaves
Have slime upon them, such as the aspic leaves
Upon the caves of Nile.
CAESAR: Most probable
That so she died; for her physician tells me
She hath pursued conclusions infinite
Of easy ways to die. Take up her bed;
And bear her women from the Monument:
She shall be buried by her Antony:
No grave upon the earth shall clip in it

A pair so famous. High events as these
Strike those that make them; and their story is
No less in pity than his glory which
Brought them to be lamented. Our army shall
In solemn show attend this funeral;
And then to Rome. Come, Dolabella, see
High order in this great solemnity.

Exeunt.

www.ingramcontent.com/pod-product-compliance
Lightning Source LLC
LaVergne TN
LVHW101946220826
846093LV00006B/126

9789388318105